Fine China

TWENTY YEARS OF EARTH'S DAUGHTERS

Fine China

TWENTY YEARS OF EARTH'S DAUGHTERS

EARTH'S DAUGHTERS / SPRINGHOUSE EDITIONS

Acknowledgements

Earth's Daughters acknowledges the support of the New York State Council on the Arts Decentralization Program administered by the Arts Council of Buffalo and Erie County.

"A shadow play for guilt" copyright 1970 by *Poems of the People* (Marge Piercy); "Kwashiorkor Bird" by Elaine Rollwagen Chamberlain reprinted from *DEBTS/A Collection of Buffalo Pieces;* "Driving for Yellow Cab" by Judith Kerman reprinted from *Aurora* #1; "Driving Across the Texas Night" by Patti Renner-Tana reprinted from *How Odd This Ritual of Harmony* (Gusto Press 1981); "Love Is When One Frees" by Jack Clarke first appeared in *Ink 6,* Just Buffalo Press; "Yes" by Thulani Davis first appeared in *Beyond Rice,* Manto Publications and Now Press; "Equal to the gods" by Ed Sanders, Just Buffalo Press, designed by Trudy and Michael Morgolis.

Printed in the United States of America

ISSN 0163-0989 - Earth's Daughters
ISBN 1-877800-04-x - Springhouse Editions

Subscriptions: $14 for 3 numbers for individuals; $22 for libraries and institutions. Available directly from Earth's Daughters.

Earth's Daughters
P.O. Box 41, Central Park Station
Buffalo, New York 14214

Springhouse Editions
76 Center Street
Fredonia, New York 14063

Fine China

TWENTY YEARS OF EARTH'S DAUGHTERS

Kastle Brill	*Frontispiece*	
Denise Levertov	*White phosphorous*	1
Marge Piercy	*A Shadow Play for Guilt*	2
Mindy Aloff	*The Stepmother Before a Banished Daughter*	4
Janet Goldenberg	*Excerpt from "Rosary" Week Two*	5
Deborah Woodard	*The Paperdolls Come Out*	6
Anne Pitrone	*Instructions for Watching a Dog Cross a Street*	6
Judy Kerman	*Galatea*	6
Miriam Palmer	*Conversations at the Love Factory*	6
Marle Matthews	*Little Woman*	6
Marie Cenkner	*Box Design*	6-7
Lillian Robinson	*Marriage*	8
Deborah Woodard	*Anti-Baby Poem*	9
Joan Colby	*The Disgrace*	10
Olga Brumas	*"Coming Out of Herself Like a Man"*	12
Colette Inez	*Misfit*	13
Lois Van Houten	*Letter to a Sister*	14
Joel Lipman	*Don't Mess with the Ladies*	15
Elaine R. Chamberlain	*Kwashiorkor Bird*	16
Diane DiPrima	*To the Patriarchs*	17
Jane Creighton	*U.S. Ships Sail Toward Vietnam*	18
lyn lifshin	*And She Doesn't Understand Why My Voice Falls Down on the Phone Fast*	20

S. Lewandowski	*Anton & Marie Lewandowski*	22
Janine M. Veto	*Mama, One, Mamma, Too*	23
Miriam Dyak	*Letter I Never Wrote My Mother*	26
Kastle Brill	*Cover Design*	27
Ada L. Houseknecht 1869-1949	*Photographs*	
Joyce Kessel	*Mama Used To Say*	28
Lillian C. Folk	*& Growing*	30
Joan Murray	*The Stowaway*	32
Pamela Gray	*To My Grandmother*	33
Judith Kerman	*from MOTHERING*	34
Tina Young	*Slaying of the Dragon*	35
L. Lee Talbert	*Revival of a Hillbilly Daughter*	36
Len Roberts	*If You'd Like*	39
Monica Stillman	*The Uses of Rage*	40
Mary Richert	*I Am My Wife*	41
Marion Perry	*Erthe's Daughters*	42
Charlotte Mandel	*Rain Window*	43
Bonnie Johnson	*Bracelet*	44
Joan Joffe Hall	*The Plate*	45
Roberta Metz	*Saga*	46
Terry Kennedy	*from A Summer Notebook*	47
Elaine Namanworth	*The Fishermen's Wives*	48
ryki zuckerman	*Illustrations for "The Fisherman's Wives"*	49
M. Rosen Fine	*Wife II & Wife IV*	50
T. Ortner-Zimmerman	*As If Anything Could Grow Back Perfect*	52
Judith Minty	*Letters to My Daughters*	53
Michael Basinski	*An Old Home*	54
Molly Evoy	*Weeping Woman*	55
Becky Birtha	*Coleus*	56
Kastle Brill	*Violent Women - Frances*	58
Kastle Brill	*Aging Ape*	59
Jimmie Gilliam	*In That House*	60
Rachel B. DuPlessis	*This room*	62

Kastle Brill	*Frontispiece for "Houses" Issue*	63
Rika Lesser	*Under the Roof*	64
Tam Lin Neville	*Waking Alone in Winter, 5 A.M.*	66
Philip Pawlowski	*Waltz in "A" Minor*	67
Linda S. Peavy	*At Stockman's*	68
Susan S. Thompson	*Crazy Ann*	69
Elizabeth Quinlan	*Outside the House*	70
Rosmarie Waldrop	*Cleaning*	72
ryki zuckerman	*Double Pillows*	73
Sy M. Baldwin	*Gloria*	74
Ellen Bass	*Sapolin Oyster White*	75
Becky Birtha	*Picking Pears*	76
Marty Cohen	*Suite M*	77
Joan E. Ford	*Junk*	80
Joel Lipman	*Origins of Poetry*	81
Gunter Werner Fuchs	*Erlernter Beruf Eines Vogels*	82
Max Wickert (translator)	*The Profession a Bird Is Educated Into*	83
Terry Kennedy	*Number 13*	84
Debbie Jenks	*Photograph (ED 10/11)*	85
lyn lifshin	*Your Manuscript We*	86
Michele Murray	*There! in the bright afternoon light*	87
Sharon Olds	*The Prisoner*	88
Sharon Olds	*Family Portrait Just Before the Tragedy*	89
Susan F. Schaeffer	*Death Is Lying Down*	90
Susan Fantl Spivak	*Paula of the Wind and the Water*	91
Jayne Lyn Stahl	*After Cleaning Ashes Off the Dresser I Sit Down to Read Artaud*	92
Linda Wagner	*The "Too-Bad-A-Woman-Doesn't-Have-Balls" Poem*	94
Kastle Brill & Robin Willoughby	*"Gee, Eddy, it's cold down here"*	95
Michele Connelly	*Snake Lying in Leaves & Grass*	96

Joan E. Ford	*A Place in the Sun*	97
Sherri Lederman	*2 Handed Shopping at*	98
	St. Lukes	
Christina V. Pacosz	*God, In Her Infinite*	100
Mary Ann Schaefer	*Wisdom, Sends Crows*	101
Joy Walsh	*To What Degree*	102
	When Does the	
Ann Fox Chandonnet	*Jacaranda Bloom?*	104
K.S. Ernst	*Florida Roots*	105
Patricia Donovan	*Linda*	106
Judith Geer	*This evening*	107
Iris Litt	*How Much Longer*	108
	Love Poem at End of	
Len Roberts	*Summer*	109
Helen Ruggieri	*Drunk in the Snow*	110
Nancy S. Schoellkopf	*15th Anniversary*	111
	After Being Rejected by	
Joanne Seltzer	*Your First Lover*	112
Conciere Taylor	*Kiss Me Goodnight*	113
Geri Grossman	*The Divorce*	114
ryki zuckerman	*Female Admitting*	116
Terry Gross &	*playback*	117
Judy Treible	*Untitled Artwork*	
Janine Canan	*They Are Riding in a*	118
	Car	
	Catherine Jackson Is	118
	Seated At The Harp	
Sally A. Fiedler	*Vicarious Experience*	119
Bonnie Johnson	*The Bird Killer*	120
Julie Kay	*My father*	121
Judith Kerman	*Driving for Yellow Cab*	122
Patti Renner-Tana	*Driving Across the*	125
	Texas Night	
Ansie Baird	*Feu D'Artifice*	126
Jack Clarke	*Love Is When One Frees*	127
Thulani Davis	*Yes*	128
Kastle Brill	*Haunted by A Dream of*	129
	Trucks (Poem Graphics)	
Dennis Maloney	*You showed me*	130
Pat Donovan	*Thor*	131

Olga Mendell	*Carla's Poem*	132
Marge Piercy	*Down*	133
Sherry Robbins	*Massaging the Perineum*	134
Joy Walsh	*The Red Cat*	136
Ed Sanders	*Equal to the gods*	138
R.D. Pohl	*Blue Baby*	140
Sam Abrams	*The Dreamtime*	145
Michael Alexander	*Workshop of the Rose*	146
Mikhail Horowitz	*Messiah*	147
Joel Lipman	*MY LOVE is*	148
Dennis Maloney	*Winter Alba*	149
Gary McLouth	*Labor Day*	150
Jack Shifflett	*tonight*	151
Joel Oppenheimer	*February*	152
Linda Haggenjos	*mer maid*	154
Nita Penfold	*Sacraments*	155
Elaine Perry	*Last Goddess on Earth*	156
Robin Kay Willoughby	*Prayer for Rain, or Something Else*	157
Robin Kay Willoughby	*Jack-In-The-Pulpit*	158
Robin Kay Willoughby	*On Public Art (Poem Graphic)*	159
Geri Grossman	*A Hymn to Mourning*	160
Li Min Hua	*Breathing Calls I've Received*	162
Li Min Hua	*8 FENCES*	164
Kastle Brill	*Summer Mass*	165
lyn lifshin	*He Said Her Bones*	166
Elaine Mott	*The Rape*	167
Penelope Prentice	*The Long Distance Lover*	168
Elise A. Bushmiller	*Li'l Tuff Guy Wear*	169
Rose Romano	*Ladies For Ferraro*	170
Susan F. Spivack	*The Objects of Dreams*	172
Judith McCombe	*Double Solstice Star*	177
Katharyn M. Aal	*Eve & Adam 1980*	178
Nancy Barnes	*Choices*	179
Jeanine Van Voorhees	*He Is Like Goldfish*	180
Bonnie Johnson	*The Prolific Poet*	182
Kastle Brill	*History*	183
Gabrielle, Maria, & Jennifer Burton	*from Litany of the Clothes*	184

Elizabeth B. Conant	*Query*	186
Thomas Kretz	*Parable 25*	187
Nita Penfold	*This Is a Poem*	188
Susanna J. Sturgis	*In Cahoots With The Fritz*	191
Camille Cox	*Portrait of Joseph Clovis Despault*	192
Kathryn Daniels	*Something to Cry About*	194
Nancy B. Friedman	*Jedediah: A Slant Rhyme*	195
Perrie J. Hill	*The Game*	196
Eileen Moeller	*1949 Pontiac*	198
Patricia Nesbitt	*Lessons*	199
Sarah Slavin	*Incest*	200
Marie Cartier	*To Her Husband*	202
Ann Fox Chandonnet	*Entering the Surroundings*	203
lola danet	*Shaman*	204
Sally A. Fiedler	*No Mercy*	205
Gary Fincke	*Poor Farm*	206
Judith Treible	*Woodcut*	207
B.A. Porte-Thomas	*Muir Woods, 1984*	208
Lily-Iona Soucie	*The Daughters of Copper Woman*	209
Janine Pommy Vega	*Atalaya*	210
Kastle Brill	*Rehearsing for War*	212
Marie Connors	*The Offspring*	213
Marilyn Kallet	*The Secret*	214
Susan Fantl Spivack	*Junkobody the Broomman*	215
Ann Goldsmith	*What Nobody Knows*	218
Lynn Martin	*A Shape Soft Enough to Wear*	219
Helen Ruggieri	*Confession*	220
Pamela Clements	*Medicine Man*	222
Gary Fincke	*Aunt Helen's Books*	223
Judith Geer	*It's Too Bad*	224
Kathryn H. Machan	*Emily Dickinson and I*	225
Leslea Newman	*Your Jacket*	226
Helen Ruggieri	*Earth:Dance*	227
Joel Lipman	*Mud of the Road*	228
Joan E. Ford	*The Meeting*	229

Fine China

TWENTY YEARS OF EARTH'S DAUGHTERS

PREFACE

Earth's Daughters has lived long enough to have developed a mythos. Part of that mythos is that if *Earth's Daughters* has a mother, that mother is Judith Kerman. Kerman gave the magazine its name, inspired by Emma Goldman's "Mother Earth." This is the root of *ED*'s name (among ourselves the mag is really ED - Ee Dee, not Ed), hence the tree logo, and both the name and the logo have been problematic from the beginning. *ED* has gotten hate mail from people who thought we were pagans, and love mail from pagans. We got reports on the status of pigs in Iowa and a lot of bad nature poetry, a lot of bad drawings of trees and of drawings of women that looked like trees.

We're proud to introduce ourselves as the longest-lived feminist publication in the United States; the first issue was published in February, 1971. A complication in that longevity is in maintaining continuity - within a commitment to diversity.

In the beginning there were three; these three editors changed, but stayed three until after issue #5/6. At that point, Judy Kerman, Lillian Robinson, and Elaine Rollwagen had each reached personal crossroads. The magazine was in stasis; none of the three wanted *ED* to die, but none could maintain it alone. Judy Kerman called a meeting of the female minds: past contributors, women involved in other publications, faculty women, women artists. She proposed that they take over *ED*, and run it as a collective. We did, and have maintained our identity as a collective ever since. Although individuals in the collective have changed as much as the magazine's format, four of the current editors were present at that original meeting. It's a miracle that a collective has survived this long, and that it functions so beautifully and audaciously. We do not allow our quality or our chutzpah to be dictated by the collective process. For more on *ED* and our process, see "The Prolific Poet," "Erthe's Daughters," and "The Meeting" in this issue.

Maybe it's because we're women, but it seems as if the writing - and the cliches - goes in cycles. Every few years, there's a flood of manuscripts, regardless of the topic. We were buried in thousands of women's *Houses*, almost all of which had dust motes dancing in the air and furnaces (in the north) or air-conditioners (in the south). Kastle Brill's black cat relieved herself on a bagful of rejected mss. (We marked the bag "DO NOT LICK SASE" after basting it with Lysol spray.) The "Mothers and Daughters" theme brought forth hordes of "strong thighs"; For the "Political" issue, we had lots of "viable candidates" and even more "second-rate wannabes." "Eye of the Beholder" brought forth so many nature poems - and corrupt-nature poems - that we decided to do an "Ecology" issue called "Lost in the Woods," for which we received too many "my-love-is-like-a-flower" poems, which was not what we meant at all.

The wonderful thing is, we got great stuff, too. Many of *ED*'s unknowns have become known. Many of our glorious writers have not, but deserve fame. This collection celebrates them all, and celebrates our collective efforts to keep it going.

Kastle Brill
ED 10/11

'White phosphorous, white phosphorus,
mechanical snow.
where are you falling?'

'I am falling impartially on roads and roofs,
on bamboo thickets, on people.
My name recalls rich seas on rainy nights,
each drop that hits the surface eliciting
the luminous response of a million algae.
My name is a whisper of sequins. Ha!
Each of them is a disk of fire,
I am the snow that burns.
                                                            I fall
wherever men send me to fall -
but I prefer flesh, so smooth, so dense:
I decorate it in black, and seek
the bone.'

Denise Levertov
ED 1

A SHADOW PLAY FOR GUILT

1.
A man can lie to himself.
A man can lie with his tongue
and his brain and his gesture:
a man can lie with his life:
but the body is simple as a turtle and straight as a dog:
the body cannot lie.
You want to take your good body off like a glove.
You want to stretch and to shrink it as you change your abstractions.
You stand in it with shame.
You smell your fingers and lick your disgust
and are satisfied.
But the beaten dog of the body remembers.
Blood has ghosts too.

2.
You speak of the collective.
You speak of open communication
but you are secret.
You form your decisions
and visit them on others
like an ax.
In all of the movement there is nothing to fear
like a man whose rhetoric is good
and whose ambition for himself is fierce:
a man who says *we,* moving us,
and means *I* and *mine.*

3.
Many people have a thing
they want to protect.
Sometimes the property is wheat, oil fields, slum housing,
plains on which brown men pick green tomatoes,
stocks in safety deposit boxes, computer patents,
maybe thirty dollars in a shoebox under a mattress.
Maybe it's a woman they own and her soft invisible labor.
Maybe it's prejudices or fermented hatred
or images from childhood of how things should be.

The revolutionary says, we can let go.
We both used to say that a great deal.
If what we change does not change us
we are playing with blocks.

4.
Always you were dancing before veiled eyes,
before the altar of guilt.
A frowning man with clenched fists
you leaned heavy as cast iron
and sucked my breasts and grappled and fed
gritting your teeth for fear
a good word would slip out:
a man who came back again and again
yet made sure that his coming was attended by pain
and marked by a careful coldness,
as if gentleness were an inventory that could run low,
as if loving were an account that would be overdrawn,
as if tenderness saved drew interest:
you are a capitalist of yourself.
You hoard for fantasies and deceptions
and the slow seep of energy out of the loins.
You fondle your fears and coddle them
while you urge others on.
They are the only reason you ever need.

I am not in your world but with my sisters.
in your world is only you
and your fantasies and your fears and your abstractions
ranged like favorite battered toys and hoarded
and the relationship you created
from what was open and alive and curious
turning it to guilt's altar
private and tight as a bankvault
or a tomb.

Marge Piercy
ED 1

THE STEPMOTHER BEFORE A BANISHED DAUGHTER

Mirror,
mirror I keep
returning. If you were
complete my face wouldn't be
broken. Glass divides us
to twins. When I see you passing through a forest,
or asleep on a rock,
your neck spread open
to the cold like the soft
throat of a bird,
I fly out of myself, finding
your absence forever
my losing. I dream
of walking into you,
the vanishing center
in you where death
heals us together.

Mindy Aloff
ED 1

ROSARY -- WEEK TWO

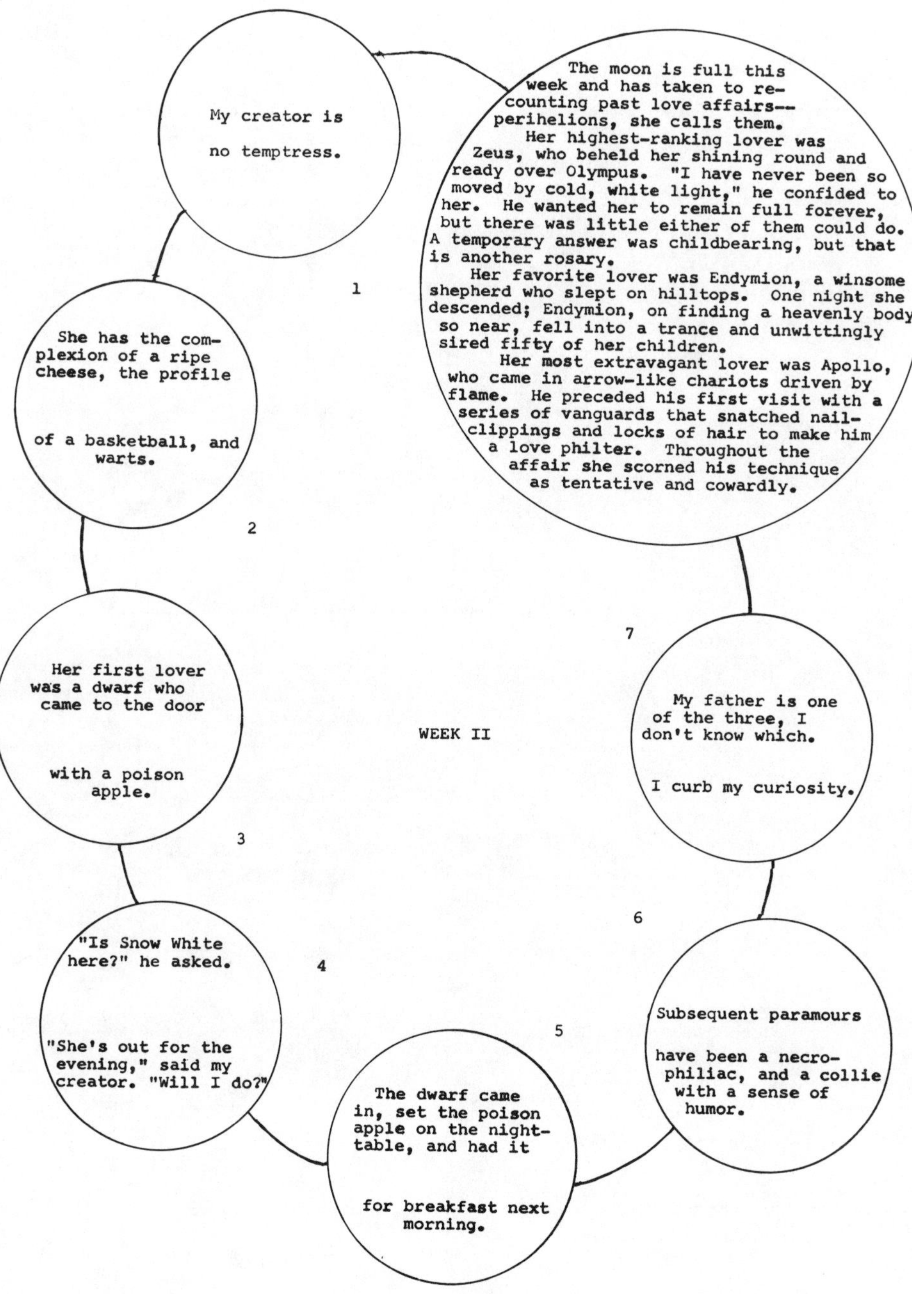

My creator is

no temptress.
1
The moon is full this week and has taken to re-counting past love affairs--perihelions, she calls them.
Her highest-ranking lover was Zeus, who beheld her shining round and ready over Olympus. "I have never been so moved by cold, white light," he confided to her. He wanted her to remain full forever, but there was little either of them could do. A temporary answer was childbearing, but that is another rosary.
Her favorite lover was Endymion, a winsome shepherd who slept on hilltops. One night she descended; Endymion, on finding a heavenly body so near, fell into a trance and unwittingly sired fifty of her children.
Her most extravagant lover was Apollo, who came in arrow-like chariots driven by flame. He preceded his first visit with a series of vanguards that snatched nail-clippings and locks of hair to make him a love philter. Throughout the affair she scorned his technique as tentative and cowardly.
She has the complexion of a ripe cheese, the profile

of a basketball, and warts.
2
7
Her first lover was a dwarf who came to the door

with a poison apple.
WEEK II
My father is one of the three, I don't know which.

I curb my curiosity.
3
6
"Is Snow White here?" he asked.

"She's out for the evening," said my creator. "Will I do?"
4
5
Subsequent paramours

have been a necro-philiac, and a collie with a sense of humor.
The dwarf came in, set the poison apple on the night-table, and had it

for breakfast next morning.

Janet Goldenberg
ED 2

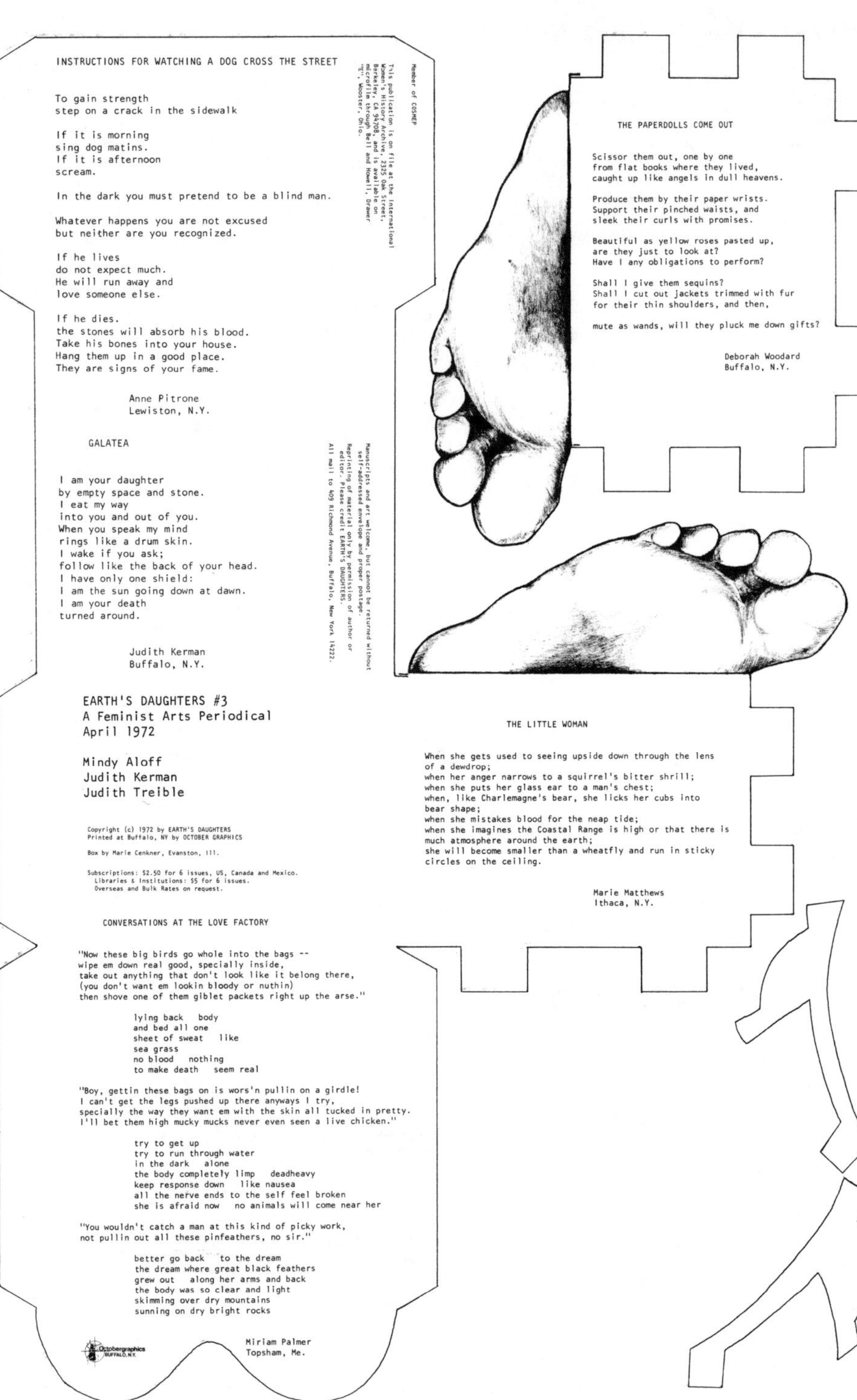

INSTRUCTIONS FOR WATCHING A DOG CROSS THE STREET

To gain strength
step on a crack in the sidewalk

If it is morning
sing dog matins.
If it is afternoon
scream.

In the dark you must pretend to be a blind man.

Whatever happens you are not excused
but neither are you recognized.

If he lives
do not expect much.
He will run away and
love someone else.

If he dies.
the stones will absorb his blood.
Take his bones into your house.
Hang them up in a good place.
They are signs of your fame.

Anne Pitrone
Lewiston, N.Y.

Member of COSMEP

This publication is on file at the International Women's History Archive, 2325 Oak Street, Berkeley, CA 94708, and is available on microfilm through Bell and Howell, Drawer "E", Wooster, Ohio.

THE PAPERDOLLS COME OUT

Scissor them out, one by one
from flat books where they lived,
caught up like angels in dull heavens.

Produce them by their paper wrists.
Support their pinched waists, and
sleek their curls with promises.

Beautiful as yellow roses pasted up,
are they just to look at?
Have I any obligations to perform?

Shall I give them sequins?
Shall I cut out jackets trimmed with fur
for their thin shoulders, and then,

mute as wands, will they pluck me down gifts?

Deborah Woodard
Buffalo, N.Y.

GALATEA

I am your daughter
by empty space and stone.
I eat my way
into you and out of you.
When you speak my mind
rings like a drum skin.
I wake if you ask;
follow like the back of your head.
I have only one shield:
I am the sun going down at dawn.
I am your death
turned around.

Judith Kerman
Buffalo, N.Y.

Manuscripts and art welcome, but cannot be returned without self-addressed envelope and proper postage.

Reprinting of material only by permission of author or editor. Please credit EARTH'S DAUGHTERS.

All mail to 409 Richmond Avenue, Buffalo, New York 14222.

EARTH'S DAUGHTERS #3
A Feminist Arts Periodical
April 1972

Mindy Aloff
Judith Kerman
Judith Treible

Printed at Buffalo, NY by OCTOBER GRAPHICS

Box by Marie Cenkner, Evanston, Ill.

Subscriptions: $2.50 for 6 issues, US, Canada and Mexico.
Libraries & Institutions: $5 for 6 issues.
Overseas and Bulk Rates on request.

THE LITTLE WOMAN

When she gets used to seeing upside down through the lens
of a dewdrop;
when her anger narrows to a squirrel's bitter shrill;
when she puts her glass ear to a man's chest;
when, like Charlemagne's bear, she licks her cubs into
bear shape;
when she mistakes blood for the neap tide;
when she imagines the Coastal Range is high or that there is
much atmosphere around the earth;
she will become smaller than a wheatfly and run in sticky
circles on the ceiling.

Marie Matthews
Ithaca, N.Y.

CONVERSATIONS AT THE LOVE FACTORY

"Now these big birds go whole into the bags --
wipe em down real good, specially inside,
take out anything that don't look like it belong there,
(you don't want em lookin bloody or nuthin)
then shove one of them giblet packets right up the arse."

lying back body
and bed all one
sheet of sweat like
sea grass
no blood nothing
to make death seem real

"Boy, gettin these bags on is wors'n pullin on a girdle!
I can't get the legs pushed up there anyways I try,
specially the way they want em with the skin all tucked in pretty.
I'll bet them high mucky mucks never even seen a live chicken."

try to get up
try to run through water
in the dark alone
the body completely limp deadheavy
keep response down like nausea
all the nerve ends to the self feel broken
she is afraid now no animals will come near her

"You wouldn't catch a man at this kind of picky work,
not pullin out all these pinfeathers, no sir."

better go back to the dream
the dream where great black feathers
grew out along her arms and back
the body was so clear and light
skimming over dry mountains
sunning on dry bright rocks

Miriam Palmer
Topsham, Me.

Octobergraphics
BUFFALO, N.Y.

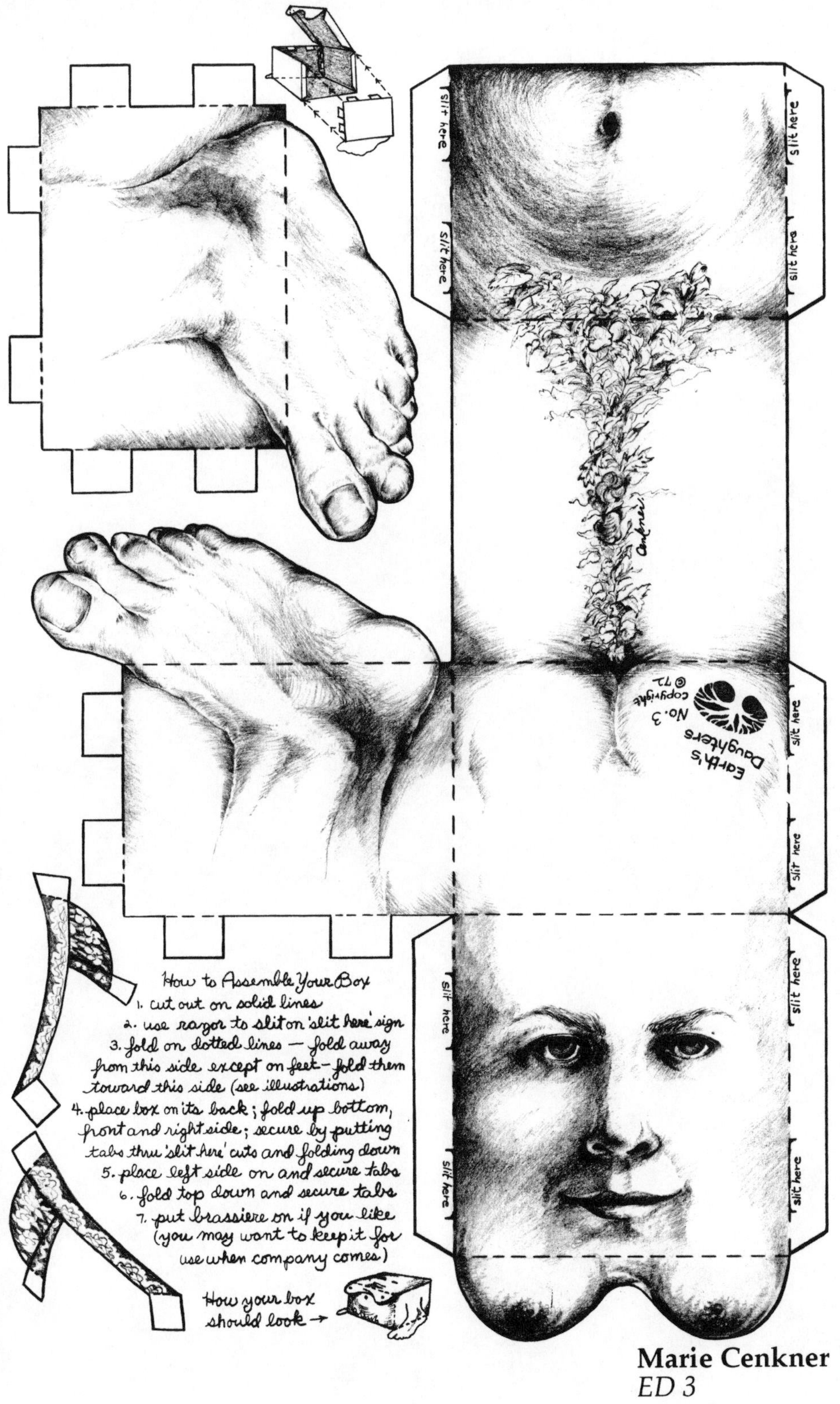

Marie Cenkner
ED 3

MARRIAGE

At the best restaurant
in Buffalo, the proprietor
is crying. Her husband's drunk,
treats her roughly in the kitchen
and, out front, blames her
for what goes wrong.
"Pretend," I tell her. "Pretend
you think
it's a joke."

Lillian Robinson
ED 4

ANTI-BABY POEM

We were burning Baby's highchair in the fire.
Baby clapped & crowed, admired sparks.
We broke her crib to splinters for the noise.
Then, she cried.
Perhaps its bars were bones,
Its creak, the pulse & tongue.
She gossiped with it while we thought she slept.

We promised her: a cloister, a boudoir, a nest.
We would braid this thing from hay
If hay were long as spun silk & never broke.
We wanted the identical pale color, with that smell.

I was pleased & thought of detached barn doors,
Lost hay & fisting roots of grass beneath soft planks
& pollen from the loft that trickles down through light.
I thought of paths in grass we pressed to hay.

Things will improve.
We'll go to the park
& sit on the benches like policemen.
I will remember the way I loved dirt & stones
& swings with poles well-anchored in cement.

Baby, sunlight of an egg,
Mulatto who has sucked the wet like fish,
Your selves digest,
You turn them in for teeth & words
& start on calcium, hard thing that holds us back.

Deborah Woodard
ED 5/6

THE DISGRACE

"we've never been women,
we've never been nobodies"
(Ancestors)
Cesar Pavese

Tough, sinewy, at eleven
I was terrified of breasts
those loose
globes of flesh
bouncing on the thin
washboard of my chest
as I set my chestnut mare
at the triple bar.

A horror
growing upon my body
like soft fists fit
for the fists and mouths of men.

Saying no, a hundred times,
I strutted,
swaggered my lean hips
in blued-out jeans,
skinny brown arms
steering the flight of geldings,
the dance of my round-rumped mare
flirting her flax tail
at the chained stud
who whickered and burned.
I spurred her past
the tangled wood
where wildflowers were snapping
from every crevice.
My narrow buttocks
settled into the rhythm of a
hand-gallop. Later
I found my first blood
crusting my thighs.
There was no hope.

I was about
to be turned into a woman,
a nobody,
a body I would live behind
that men would want for its own sake,
for its bubble breasts
and jiggly thighs.

I ran my hands
over my flat-muscled flanks
toughening against
the desire to cry out
like a weak creature,
a woman, a nobody.

Joan Colby
ED 5/6

"COMING OUT OF HERSELF LIKE A MAN"

for j

"like" won't do it jan
nice
japanese lanterns around it all

& a sense of awe
filling out what don't
make a man in the first
place anyway (right?)

"like" won't do it
though the first time it happens you blink
& the second you think now
i know
& the third you pick up some tamps on
the way & forget it it goes on
happening

"like" don't do it

we've had more likes than you'd fit in
your father's barn
more likes than men &
more men than women but
none of them did
the trick

coming out "like" is a bastard
a man doesn't come
out - he slips

Olga Brumas
ED 5/6

MISFIT

What multiplication tables I ate
to memorize the grades.
I, a passing girl,
promoted into breasts,

even rehearsed the wedding aisle
but on my stage just short of vows,
the bride passed out; she carried a house,
its burden of meals.

My school of advice
was semestered in clouds.
M I S F I T, the skywriter wrote
above my roof. I was stuck in a box
of popular tunes

not listening to attention signs
in failing red
the masters assigned to my chart.

I dreamed they found a gangster's moll
under my smile, a sadistic gun
cocked in my heart
where submit, survive were billed
as a band and I needed a beat
to live out the dance.

Quandry hall was my domain.
I chewed on my thighs and sewed up the pain.

Moral:

Don't pity the eagle trapped in a coin,
remember his double near the gold egg sun.

Better to crack like a hundred year egg
served to a feast
than to sit on your legs like a frozen bird
in the nest of your grief.

Colette Inez
ED 5/6

LETTER TO A SISTER

Write me a letter of bone
of girth and body brew
of beating heart muscle
and breaking breath of joy.
A touch / the brush
of young, resilient birch
a blink of eye...faster
than a Goshawk's fall
a laugh / hearty as a harvest
pumpkin.
In short : send to me
yourself / long-legged
and fully pouched
as a Heron
stamped in a prominent place
perishable : this article
cannot be returned.

Lois Van Houten
ED 5/6

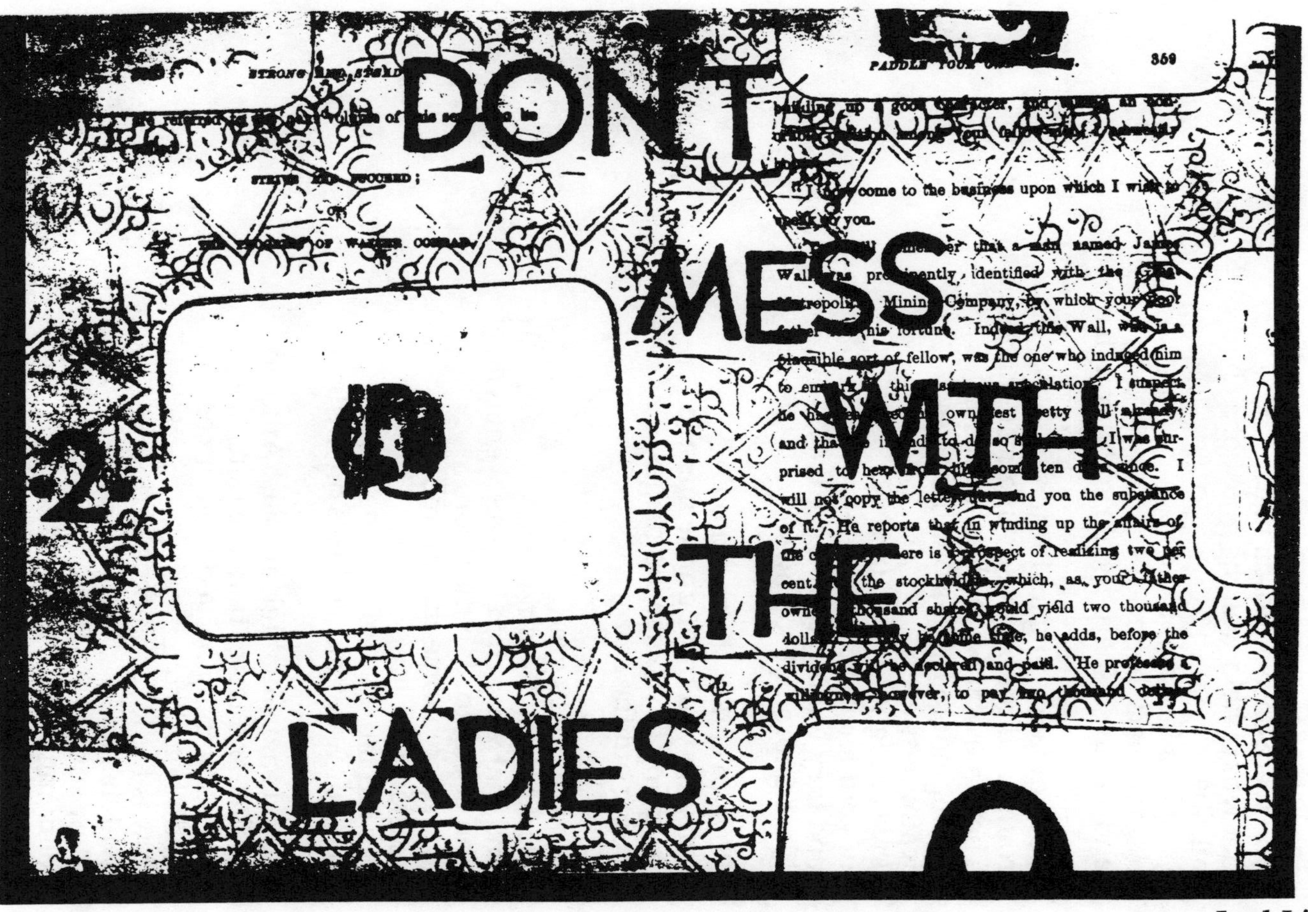
DON'T
MESS
WITH
THE
LADIES

Joel Lipman
ED 24

KWASHIORKOR BIRD

Before the rain
the Father told me
you were once almost a man
but what I held was the ghost of a child
all ribs
dangling feet and hands
a small black head
and a chin so sharp it cut right through me.

Your monkey fingers fluttered
round and round these American buttons.
They said you were almost a man.
Trying not to touch your fleshless
featherless arms
I was caught in the curve
of your air-light femurs
and they wound round my waist
like an apron of sorrows.

It was a child's game Antonio
carrying you through the mission
laughing in strange languages
riding out the storm.

But your eyes grew dark
blacker than the sky
and that was when my feet went wild
and began to slap the floor
with a cry worse than thunder
masking the limp
tap tap tap
of your water blown heels on my back.

And I said sing high and fast Antonio
higher and faster than the rain.
For something moved in your chest
and I heard it.
It was the kwashiorkor bird
with his low
slow song
of dying.

Elaine Rollwagen Chamberlain
ED 7

TO THE PATRIARCHS
(for Inez Garcia)

> *"That a man's body is*
> *in itself a weapon in a*
> *way that a woman's body*
> *is not."*
> **Free Inez Garcia Committee**

My body a weapon as yours is
MY CHILDREN WEAPONS ETERNALLY
My tits weapons against the immaterial

My strong thighs
 choking the black lie
My hips
 haven & fort
 place where I stand
 & from which I fight

My war is concentrated in the noise
 of my hair
My hands
 lethal to imprecision
My cunt a tomb exploding
 yr christian conscience

My teeth tear out the throat of yr despair
My jaws annihilate computer centuries
My arms/my knees embrace yr serpent
 yr sin becomes my song

The shock waves of my pleasure
 annihilate
all future shock
all future shock forever

Diane DiPrima
ED 7

U.S. SHIPS SAIL TOWARD VIETNAM

lost or alone
we can't tell /
a young woman finds words
to reply

for Margaret Randall

& vivid as all else
as the corner of the room before me
my parents' death & departure
Gouldie lovely father's friend
comes crying through the door
& I cry this again
all that I know

it's a gray dream
I suck my hands
dead I don't see them
in my world
we don't look

& then she has me
by this tail
pulls me outright
through Hanoi tough /
particular like

I'd have her
in that region I've learned to avoid
that sexual, rich & struggling region
that is my body
these deadly parents
that is Hanoi /

no, one could say
it never happened
they never succumbed to it
one could say in time we'll forget

but she has me
no way out
of my desire
the lovely purple bruise
pours through all my surfaces
this is to tell me I've been hit
I've been a stranger
confined & enchanted
powder in my ears

walk me around
kiss me
I'm not so pretty
tell me again
about the long Vietnamese hair

sing them
the names not like
mother   father
but names I can't say
words for survival
the 27 new ways to say *bomb*
as we know the weather also
to be various
& moving

or Ha Tinh, Hong
how I could say *I want you*
if I had to /
when I wanted

or how I could /
inhabit a nation

Jane Creighton
ED 7

AND SHE DOESN'T UNDERSTAND WHY MY VOICE FALLS DOWN ON THE PHONE FAST

i take the phone off
the hook if there's
any man on the brown
bed   somehow she
knows   but tries
all night gets me
bleary eyed in the
morning   she says
she was worried nags
did i eat how if i
feel depressed its
because i haven't
then she knocks my
boy friend's braids
says he's got greedy
fingers wants me for
my house she thinks
he's plotting with
his old girl moans
how much better the
ones who i let go
and she tells me the
man she said was a
copper when i was
wanting his fingers
is going back to
his wife and how she
got blonde and thin
she says that money
is all that and how
i ought to go to
the doctor call a
man to fix the plug
before my boyfriend
steals my money

and why can't i get
up there thanksgiving
without him   If i
don't i may have to
buy my soup and
she says you know
you're so important
she says love how
i mean to that i'm
only down because
i don't think enuff
of myself

lyn lifshin
ED 8

ANTON & MARIE LEWANDOWSKI

Grandfather handled steel as
roller-man in the Tonawanda mills.
Introduced my father to the men on his shift
"This is my youngest son Stanley"
& gave him a quarter to bring a pail
of beer from the corner tavern
to wash down their tin box lunches.
I only remember him
as a slight man in skivvies,
rumors of his long dying &
my father coming back to the car-
face gone pale, blue eyes set.
But memory can only affirm the past
& I want no such affirmation.
I know my life flows.
I can no more bring you to life again
than I could calm my fear of your wife,
Marie my grandmother, who spoke Polish
too loud, too quick, would grab at me.
She was crying; she wanted to hold
her grand-child to her breast.
Blood of her blood. Blood of my blood.
What caused that shrinking?
I was raised in another place,
another time, among cold people.
Coolness haunts me grandmother. Cure me.
Hold me. When was the last time I saw you?
Blood whispers through my dreams.
It has a life of its own, which I ask
my share of. Speak to me, my heart.
I'll understand where the words come from.

S. Lewandowski
ED 8

MAMA, ONE, MAMMA, TOO

I.

your flecked old hands
quiver threading a needle
Mama, I suppose
I'll inherit that lace banquet cloth
ringed with cherubs
I never saw you use
along with the painfully precise
family files and photo albums
I saw you fondle
through the years
you called me a "Chosen Child"
and have the papers and memories
to prove it

II.

they say we have similar gestures
you packed my balanced lunch
using six staples and a rubber band,
writing my name on three sides
last name, first name, middle initial

period
you packed me in snowsuits
puffing me up to a Zeppelin
immobile on my varnished sled
with safety runners
on snow capped ant hills
I bet you wished you could have
packed my knees together, too
Mama, I know
you gave me a sturdy bra
but what about the watermelon breasts
of ladies on playing cards Papa kept
behind the bar and
puffed out women smiling in public
admitting all

?

III.

they say we're similar through the eyes...
yours are Alp ice blue
within the waltz city of your nativity
the green of mine does not root
in suburban lawns   swamp sources are more likely
or spiral smoke rings from a hookah
floating in illusion
you were proud of the budding scholar
ruining my eyes reading under covers
six years old? what age?
Mama, I was getting fucked over
a thousand times   carried down rivers
becoming a mystic
within those womb warm walls
cross legged on the white colonial bedspread
in the dust free cubicle
I crawled
through the gutters of port towns
ripped by briny lovers

IV.

they say I have another name
different than the one on my lunchbags
and the diplomas and awards and certificates
you have tenderly fitted and framed
thank you
for my childhood
I think thank   I suppose
for your pragmatic legacy and Lysol halls
I stare at your tidy body
plummeting for some recessed pool that can
explain my undulations
some hoped for fire
to melt this Golden Girl from a craven image
back to the crucible
where
I was conceived
back even further
the forbidden frozen instant
when unsanctioned assent crazed the air

V.

she carried me full nine moons
Mama
from that second
yes
delivering me safely to your stability
with relief, with regret, repulsion
I will never know
how
you sit across the room
mending a cherub, Mama
mindful of thrift
the value of a good name
you smile across
to your tastefully upholstered daughter
whose
swamp eyes shroud:
vision of vacant Alps
packed under a cloud

Janine M. Veto
ED 8

LETTER I NEVER WROTE MY MOTHER

We have been sleeping with our heads to the North several weeks now - things are better. The days taste primitive, the past is not dead or safe to live in. We eat millet as though it were an offering to make the leaves turn.

Bruce takes my words and cuts them into soundless shapes that have a strange uncommunicative grace in them. We think again about wanting babies, knowing even our wood and poems can't hold their own against this life. I have no more explanations.

But if you come to visit me this winter, I'll show you rooms with branches hanging from the ceilings, streets leading lost identities in the snow, inlets no different from cornfields, sleeping side by side with them. I'll take you to the Russian town where the old women wear babushkas, their faces folded like stocking dolls, and show you the fairy-tale house where I could live one life. We can have tea and pirozhki - I won't tell you anything, just smile and wave my hands. Everything is there, Mother, you have to catch the images as they pass, like bubbles I used to blow at you, balloons. I am the Balloon Lady, Mother, on the corner. The balloons are everycolor with pictures of castles and black cats, lovers and sunsets. I am the Balloon Lady wrapped in three brown skirts like beetle's wings, a blue scarf tied in my hair. I am the Balloon Lady, pigeons dance at my feet.

Miriam Dyak
ED 8

ADA L. HOUSEKNECHT

mama used to say
don't rock babe
its distractin
so i tried hard to sit still
sat on my hands
kept my legs together
& kept quiet
like little girls
suppose to

but then
in the hot sticky nite
it would start again
& i would
rockaway
the darkness and the dragon

& mama used to say
don't rock babe
its annoyin
so i tried again so hard
sat with my hands folded
& my knees together
sittin as still
as i could
& kept quiet
on the outside
like good girls do
but then
in the cold lonely nite
itd come again

& i would
rockaway
the cold and the unknown

& mama used to say
don't rock girl
it aint right
so i sighed
& i tried to sit proper
hands in my lap
& knees together like they
should be
& kept quietly humming
to myself
thinkin bout what other girls do

but then
in the middle of the nite
there itd be

& i would
rockaway
the fear & all alone

& mama used to say
cant do nothin
with her no more
devils got her

& i would just sit
rockin

Joyce Kessel
ED 8

& GROWING

Ambition: To grow
        netted   insidious as root hairs   over the stone
        keening, whetted   against it.
Trial strengthening   strength trying
        flint searching   stone walls struck for sparks
Mother is the resource of invention.

That which we battle, we become   and overcome.
Only time reveals the truth of the pendulum's path
        which reveals time.

Those biding spots   isolated   unnoticed   over the globe:
                Switzerland   Belgium   Montenegro

Lessons of the confessional: Heaven burns like hell.
Lessons of the scullery: each knife has its own best purpose.
Lessons of the nursery: connect the dots.

whistling   and steaming   with the tea
Learning the ways of herbs   and of seasons,
                                        Oil of Wintergreen Hollyberry
                                        May   March   August
                                        & waiting

Learning the values of spice and diversity
        (involuntary   but ingenious)
        the matriarch's secrets   strange pastes
strange charms
                                        mustard seed   quinine
henna
        using kuchen to thwart kinder
                                        & counting
& multiplying   & adding   & growing
                                        & growing

Epics in shoeboxes
Epics on the backs of recipes

Burning witches provoked   evoked   in seance together
        fashioning   each from her unfashioned self
                a bit of the 47*th* coil, the Z
        passed down
        hidden   with the recipes   in the shoeboxes
                          pressed in the family Bible
Evolving   warranted   and opportune

& growing.

Lillian C. Folk
ED 8

THE STOWAWAY

Under your eyelid
at night
you carry the child
who never was:
three inches,
a piece of liver,
still dropped by a doctor
in a wastecan.

Years after,
a schoolgirl in rosaries,
I perfect your guilt:
"you should have baptized"
your sliver liver child,
forever in limbo,
cannot get out,
can't climb to heaven
from a wastecan.

Can you love a child
the size of a seed,
an unfolding leaf
that would fit
the palm of your hand?
Or did you drop
a thread in some design
that can never be recovered?

"I will not have children,"
you mourned,
gave birth a year later,
a year later
I came.
My sister-brother
thrown back
too small
still swims into our minds.
Had it lived,
we know,
I would not be here.

Joan Murray
ED 8

TO MY GRANDMOTHER

My mother has a box
in her kitchen
filled with the gadgets
you gave her.
Five hundred miles
away, in my kitchen
there's a drawer full
of gadgets, the ones
my mother wouldn't use
but couldn't throw away.
Between her and me
there's a network
of gadgets,
we're connected by
an indoor clothesline
a soft boiled egg opener
a hard boiled egg slicer
a three bladed onion chopper
a five hour timer
a clam opener
an ice cracker
an ice crusher
a garlic presser
and a lemon squeezer.
Your gadgets,
your bargains,
the gifts you passed out
like candy, those tiny ways
to make life easier,
these are our keepsakes,
our heirlooms.

Pamela Gray
ED 8

from MOTHERING

Alwin always knows the answers to everything . she makes herself an owl on a branch . the wind moves the tops of the trees . she slicks a feather, patience, something is coming, she is as still as the rocks . heartbeat pounding he doesn't see her, she is on his back, claws pulling into his shoulders, stomach, he is down on the ground screaming and trying to pull away . answer this, you bastard! answer me! oh, he is smiling again, so condescendingly: I'm sorry it isn't clear to you, my dear; let me put it another way

Judith Kerman
ED 9

SLAYING OF THE DRAGON

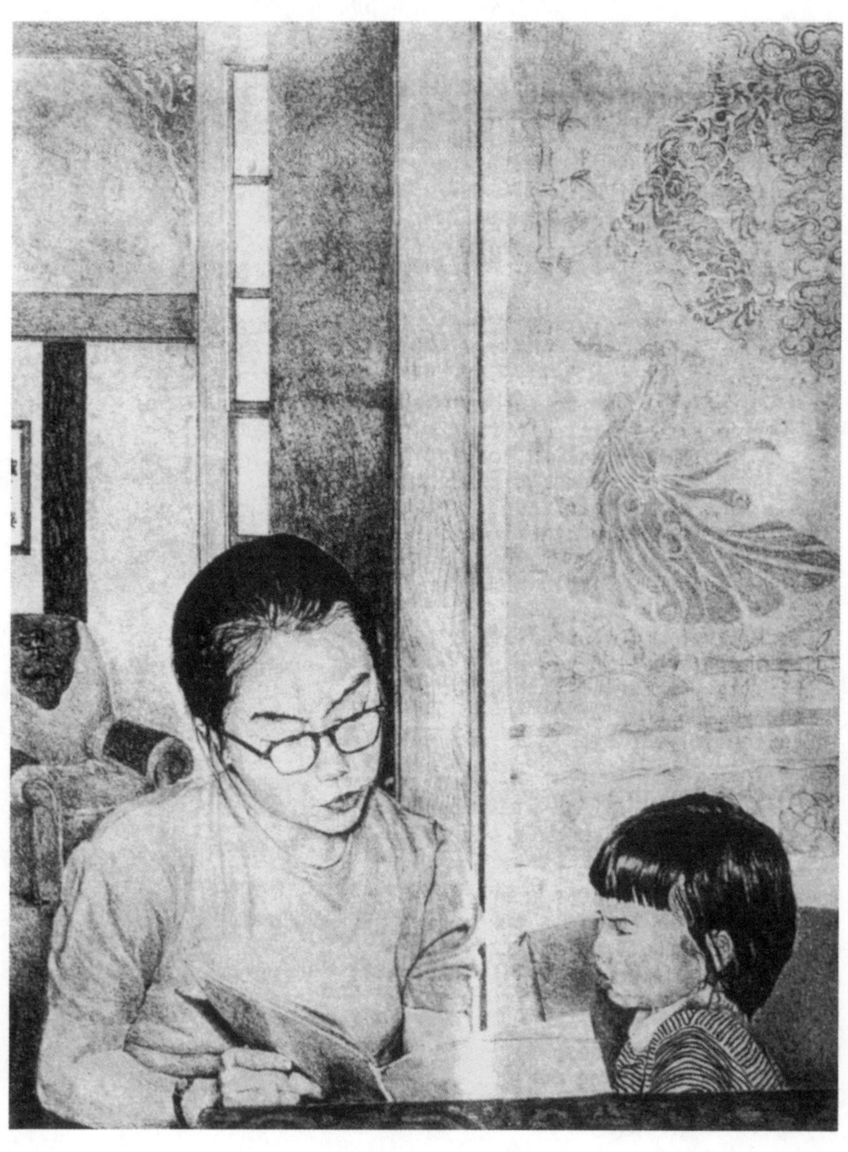

Tina Young
ED 10/11

REVIVAL OF A HILLBILLY DAUGHTER

For Ntozake Shange who helped
me recall that I'm a daughter
of the Appalachians

daddy?
say daddy are ya liss'nin?
member when ya did this thang
a layin ona hands?

'cept it waz'n a healin time
but a ritual jus the same

boozin' man
drinkin mash and bayin at the moon
skillet cross ma back
  burn'n fire
bottle on ma head
  crack'n blue light'nin

broom handle
ramin me an
ramin me
  splinterin all up on ma center
        while crawlin lika dog
        crashin down stairs
  lickin ma wounds
too afirt to scream
too afirt to cry

an ma baby afloatin somewhere
ina West Virginia sewer
inta memry

daddy
becha didn know
couldin know
you'd abin a grandaddy?

but aincha gran
jus the same
with a layin ona hands
  a crying in the night
  totin a gun
        shootin the chrissmas tree
        aimin at me
  an feelin lika man
with a layin ona hands
a layin ona hands

daddy?
say daddy are ya liss'nin?
member when ya did this thang
a layin ona hands?

i dun some layin ona hands my own self
gentle hands
lovin but lyin hands
gazin inta brown eyes blue eyes
alla time seein them red eyes
an laffin in yer face

'cept it waz'n a healin time
but a ritual jus the same

but i'm dun strokin strangers
makin a joke a myself
  an yer silent apology wud be acceptid
  'cept sorry ain't enuf
        er nessarry

did alota layin ona hands
alota layin ona hands
an now that i'm growd
bin meanin to ask:
  why dincha ever touch me
        daddy?
daddy?
say daddy are ya liss'nin?
member when ya did this thang

a layin ona hands?
well daddy
sorry daddy
ain't yer mamatoo dam tired to be yer child
  the day dun give way
  so the nite cud live
cuz daddy
I kin cry now
an alla ma tears
washed me clean
an dowsed the fire
in the sun

an I thank ya for
yer layin ona hands
made me strong
give me vision

an I see the light atha moon
  ridin lone cross the sky
        smilin down on me
              witha layin ona hands
        creatin ma own shadow
  now
  now
  now

L. Lee Talbert
ED 10/11

IF YOU'D LIKE

If you'd like we could sit on the redwood porch
 this afternoon
and watch the dead things start trying to grow
or watch the sun moving on the willow or
melting the icicles.
If you cross your legs I may think
of other women
or their eyes in various lights
and their desires.
If you remain perfectly still
you may be a statue again
your straight nose
your thin lips
the fine blonde hair
moving slightly/the only thing
bringing you alive again.
I don't know how we got here
so don't ask
your fingers shaking violently
wrapped around the heavy porcelain cup
because this is February
and there's no evergreens to block the wind
from blowing cold on our bare skin.

Len Roberts
ED 10/11

THE USES OF RAGE

She decides she's had enough,
gets down the tub and washboard
to clean her mind.
She drags it back and forth
across the blank metal lines,
to force our the irritations,
coarse black burrs,
to squeeze out
the greasy rage.
Soon her hands are coated with fury
like vaseline,
clear and clinging,
and sniffing at her fingers,
she rubs it on her mouth, her tongue.
She spreads the unguent
on her breasts - how soothing -
so she continues,
smearing her belly, her thighs,
and discovering
that between her legs
it melts, and lubricates.
Now she begins to dance,
gleaming with anger,
smooth and mad,
and no one
can hold her still.

Monica Stillman
ED 10/11

I AM MY WIFE

I am my wife
I slip and tell stories that embarrass me
I burn the coffee and choke on it
My curlers poke and stab me in the night.

My celibacy can be explained by the fact that
I simply refuse to cheat on myself

Oh, often I'll complain about my bad habits
but it's understood that secretly
I adore me.

Because I am my wife
Every day is my anniversary
Even death cannot part me.

Mary Richert
ED 10/11

ERTHE'S DAUGHTERS

(for Judy Kerman July, 1978)

There are problems
  in leaving a seven-year-old
Even with such carefully chosen
                foster parents
Can they be counted on
  when she needs twenty-four-hour care
Or will they be diverted by children of their own?
  What will they answer strangers
        when asked about her name,
                her history
  Will she be properly dressed
        when she goes to press?

Will she, herself, be difficult, always saying
  "this is how my mother did it"
Will she pine for her mother
  or her mother for her?

Perhaps the new parents will not get along
                with each other
  each wanting the upper hand,
              the final say
in how she is raised
  each demanding tokens
              of special affection.

They will at least
              when her mother visits
              parade her
        have her bow and curtsy
 show off her manners and talents
and say
        "Look how well
        We have done with her
        Isn't she lovely now?"

Marion Perry
ED 10/11

RAIN WINDOW

rain
leaves
oak
& hickory
one
green brimming
the glass field

sky
a linen screen
clear
light threading
in webs of leaf
                                        by leaf
    inside
my eyes
are sieves
the sky wrung close
the lawn steams

Charlotte Mandel
ED 10/11

BRACELET
(for Babs)

in my dream you hold it
over your hand, the
silver-edged stones linked
one by one/mahogany
satin dark
against your skin

the warm brown
ripples light and
dark, reflecting
display cases polished
hanging plants jade and
turquoise/calm
and quiet

choose, you say
the light
on your
palm, the
tiger eyes

Bonnie Johnson
ED 10/11

THE PLATE

For the second night in a row
she awakens from a dream
of sitting in a pool of blood.

In her dream her husband
was unchanged after long analysis;
"Don't expect me to be faithful,"
he says over and over.
"When you learn to give,"
she asks, speaking to him
or herself, "what do you get?"

Back in kindergarten they kept a log.
Her entry: "I get tired waiting."
It's hard to tell the stillborn
from new life.

While she washes breakfast dishes
her fingers play the soap bubbles;
warm water brings back
her dream.
She fishes for the cracked plate
she hates and smashes it,
but it is the wrong plate and she cannot
yet trust herself to break another.

If you give, she thinks, you get
the illusion of virtue;
if you get, the illusion of power.

Today her horoscope advises
"expel what is aborted."

She tells her husband she has made up
her mind. A lot could happen.
Tonight she dreams she stands
on a platform, her arm is light,
when she shakes it
feathers grow, and wings.

Joan Joffe Hall
ED 10/11

SAGA

He had two ex-wives, four children
and a television.

He turned on the television.

Roberta Metz
ED 10/11

from A SUMMER NOTEBOOK

1.
I miss you.
I miss the white peony
sitting in the crystal vase
placed like a miniature chaperone between us.

I remember the gypsy
saying that you would go
on a long voyage and that I would travel

nowhere. That you would travel with friends,
a dozen maybe. That I would stay
home and talk

to no one in particular. My friends
only a few. The gypsy
looked at me

with tears in her eyes. Your hand held mine.
Your leg pressed against my jeans.
I unpeeled

a $10 bill
from my husband's skin.
He paid for the gypsy's prophecy that says
I'll be yours before Winter eats away the ice

of my bones.

Terry Kennedy
ED 10/11

THE FISHERMEN'S WIVES

The fishermen's wives
Smelling of seablood and foam
Have exchanged their pink cheeks
And feathered hair
For the heads of fish
Their breasts
Once circles of soft and shimmer
Have turned into fins
Scaly and wet with salt-milk

The women
Whose husbands are fishermen
Grow green and cold in nets
All they know of moonlight
Is that it moves the tides
And causes their deep fish parts
To drip bright red brine

The wives of magicians
Make love inside of top hats
And turn into rabbits
Before the third act
While executives' wives
Attach leather handles
To their shoulders
And give birth to paper children

Praise to the doctor's wife
Who heals herself

God bless
The mortician's wife
Who lives forever

Elaine Namanworth
ED 10/11

ILLUSTRATIONS FOR "THE FISHERMAN'S WIVES"

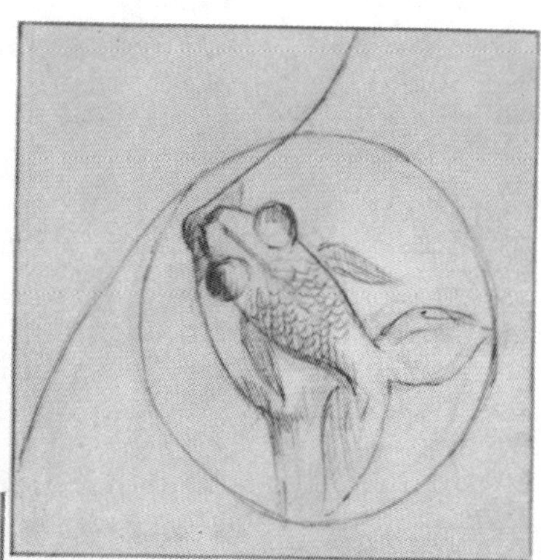

ryki zuckerman
ED 10/11

WIFE II

She goes out wearing his sox
his suit his hair on her lip
as a clue for others
that she's there as
Missus Minus his who.

(you know who: her)

They say day after day
"did you see my red thing, my glass thing, my big thing?"
Her eye computes the places with things on them.
For irreplaceables: that lady no one can do without!

Her moments collect upon the air-conditioning grille.

The butcher asks if she's as well as she was
calling her by another name
and she exits knowing she must begin again
the expensive purchase of her identity.

Her forces move centrifugally
she sends out rubberbands of action
she sends out Christmas cards
she sends out the laundry
she sends out one child w/lunch
she sends out signals of stress
(signs of slipping) (S.O.S.)

If, at two tomorrow,
beneath beautifying machines,
she reads, "The Bulletin for Atomic Scientists",
instead of "Vogue"
and says of her iridescent nails, "clip them"
and walks out on the movie of her life,

will the audience wait?

WIFE IV

She told me that he sat sat sat
for fifteen years like a pumpkin
silent at his meals silent
and went out from her life
like a light
god

she told me that she talked talked talked
and her words bounced back at her
problems in math
she was never good at math
why wasn't she?

he visits every other weekend
he's taken a small apartment
on the east side
he's found a slim girl
young, daring, very bright
he's got plenty of money now that
he's 35
god

I'll have it different
listen to me planning for it
like college or marriage
or kids
the coming together
the coming apart
but I'll be the one to go
get a job take a studio
write
I'll be the one
He'll have to worry about
the kids
the dentist, home from work
when there's a fever
hire some grey lady
or some student
pretty, needing the protection
maybe he'll marry her
or leave her
I'll visit every other weekend

God!
I'll have stopped being his best friend.

M. Rosen Fine
ED 10/11

AS IF ANYTHING COULD GROW BACK PERFECT

These days
I spend all day
burning my past
watching sheets of paper
shoot up in orange flames.
                    There is less and less I wish to say.
                    Much of what I said was useless.

I study a single stone
its purity of line
shimmering in the heat
set grape ivy
in the sun
keep the soil moist
feed the cats.

I give away everything I consider unnecessary
to someone who may use it.
I try to learn to live with less than less.

Toni Ortner-Zimmerman
ED 12

LETTERS TO MY DAUGHTERS

This week I received two love letters,
one from a boy still in high school, another
from an older man in his twenties,
a man who whispers about mountains.
Your father doesn't read my mail. He pretends
disinterest in the postmarks, the crimped penmanship,
the shy poems folded inside.
Even when it mattered, he never wrote me. I think he was
embarrassed by misspelled words, stammering lines.
But now he watches me as I watch
for the mailman's truck. He notices
how my fingers stain the curtains when I part them,
that I float through snow in my bathrobe to the mailbox.
I hide the letters in dark drawers and pull them out
when I can't remember my name. They smell like wild
violets.
Your father? Lately, I find him bent at his desk,
hands knotted over blank papers. I must tell him
those young men are only in love with poetry.

Judith Minty
ED 13

AN OLD HOME

where I once
lived
          the house
empty
there is nothing
in her heart of me
it is morning
          and clear
the windows are
broken

Michael Basinski
ED 14/15

WEEPING WOMAN

Pale windows are cackling.
Door jambs jab her between the knees.

Long fingers fan slitted eyes
whose black light lathers
in red leather lines.
Hands fold in prayer
but defy at the joints.

The overwhelming greyness of the pavement.
The odd strut of black birds
in a puddle of a trash lid.

The panorama pared down to a point.

Molly Evoy
ED 14/15

COLEUS

Once we decided to live together,
I began to make compromises.

"I have so many plants," I said apologetically.
"I don't know where they all will fit."
You thought I should give some of them away.
"I grew them because I wanted them."

And the coleus grew wild and abundant
In the west window:
I had never cut it back.
I refused to subject it to compromise, to control.

We began to paint and move furniture.
I made arrangements to give up my apartment,
Promised my chest of drawers to friends,
Painted my bookcase a color you liked.
I measured the tiny windows of the new apartment,
Measured the boxes I had collected for plants.
Still, the coleus thrived,
Crowding against the window frame,
Spilling joyfully across the curtains.

When the day came to move the plants
I took my sewing scissors
And deliberately chopped off all the green.
Purple juice ran down the silver blades.
I didn't save the pieces:
You said we would have no room
For more plants, in the new house.
And the amputated coleus fit
Into the right-sized section of the box
With all the other plants.

Now you tell me you've changed your mind.
You don't want to live with me after all.
Again I am moving furniture
Unpacking boxes
Like a film rewinding, all backwards and wrong.
You walk away carelessly
As if you've just avoided a near-accident.
And I am left
Like the coleus
Some kind of mutilated sacrifice.

Becky Birtha
ED 14/15

VIOLENT WOMEN

Frances

Held as a home crasher,
held for attempted murder,
Mrs. Pedrosi,
Age 42
Tried to kill her husband
and an unidentified female,
age 28,
by driving a station wagon
through the picture window
of the livingroom,
at the condominium
she once occupied
with Mr. Pedrosi,
age 47.

One count...Assault,
with a deadly weapon,
suburban car-pool
child-bearing,
wooden-bodied weapon.

Two counts...Attempted Murder.
Backed the car
Out past the couch,
Past the piano with the children's pictures,
to try again in third.

Three counts...
Reckless endangerment,
Destruction of property,
Attempted suicide.

Kastle Brill
ED 14/15

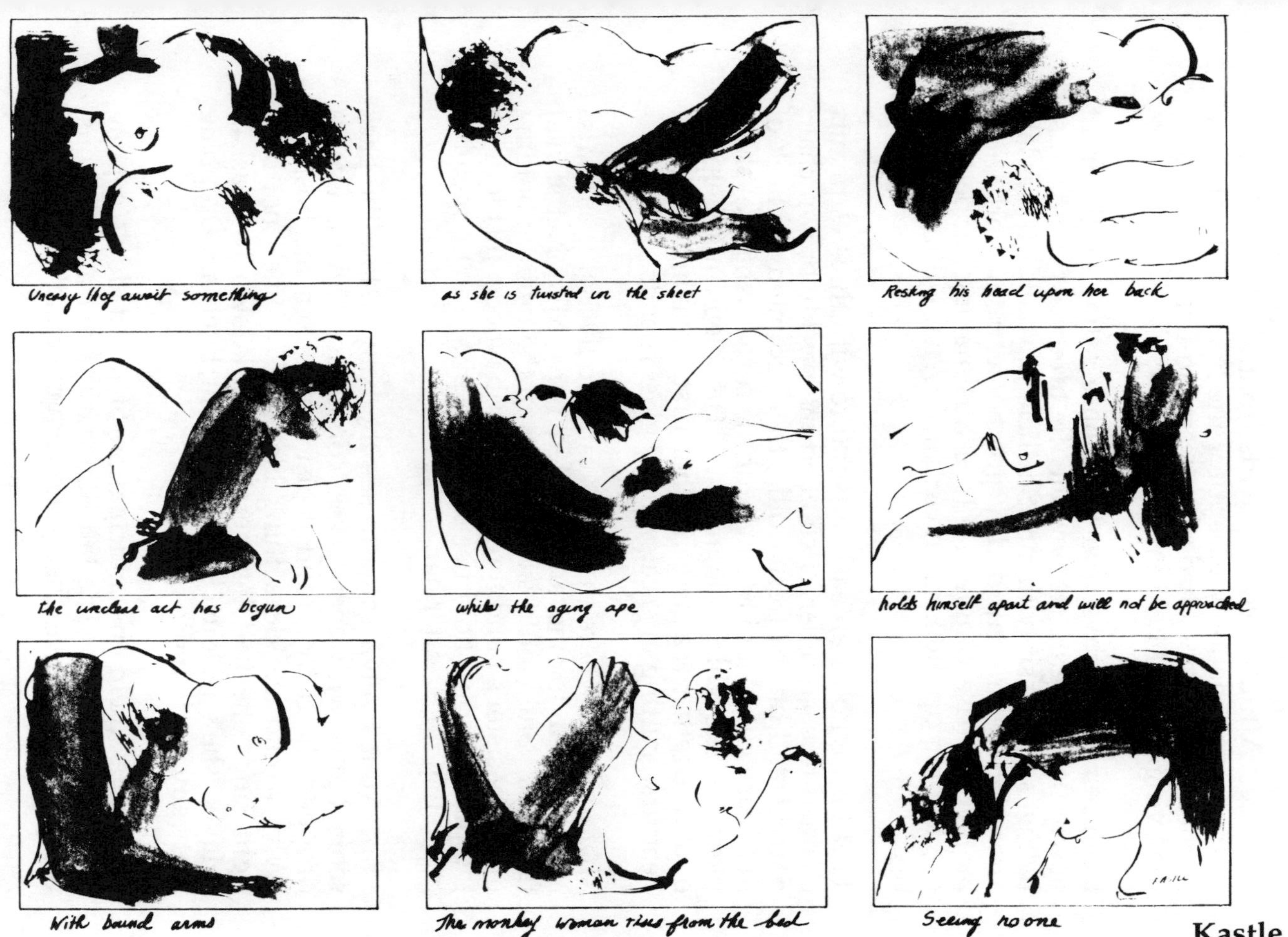

Uneasy they await something
as she is twisted in the sheet
Resting his head upon her back
the unclear act has begun
while the aging ape
holds himself apart and will not be approached
With bound arms
The monkey woman rises from the bed
Seeing no one

Kastle Brill
ED 10/11

IN THAT HOUSE

That house emerges through flakes of time: Pennsylvania Avenue. A full welcoming wide front porch. The rooms of the house shadowy except for the living room and the kitchen. My parents' bedroom seems to float from behind the living room. My room is obscure.

I can remember myself at that house sitting on the front newly painted grey steps while the firetrucks came. Miss Bell was told to sit with me. She held my hand. It was late afternoon before my daddy got home from work. My mother's grease caught fire (she was making supper) the fire leaping up the kitchen curtains. What will my daddy say?

That house holds an early adventure with three elephants chained to each other. I climbed the prickly brown chair, dared stand on the fresh doilie, then mounted the back of this "easy chair" and reached for the corner what-not shelf, place of the china elephants. The elephants helpless bound together reached the floor first, breaking. I landed headfirst, cutting my scalp on my glass friends.

That house is where that baby came to live with us. Miss Nettie loved Joanne and spoiled her. Miss Nettie had favorites. She would sit for hours in the twilight holding my baby sister's hand through the crib woods. Just four, in the photograph I hold her proudly - but I can't remember me in that house after her.

. . . . Aunt Evelyn came to see the baby. Now the back room lights with energy. A commotion. Aunt Evelyn dropped the baby - and it just home from the hospital! "Why would she do a thing like that?" "She's not been right since she had her nervous breakdown in Alaska." "Maybe she's jealous?" I liked Aunt Evelyn. Dropping that baby made sense to me.

That house held the anticipation of my daddy's coming home from work. The tall thin darkhaired man, serious, whose black eyes laughed - shone in my child's memory like the Christmas star. My daddy tossed the blond bubbles of my hair high over his strong face and confronted his father in my somber blue eyes. In that house with that baby there, I turned to my daddy. Each day's clock turned on his coming home. Facing the depths of the child in me, I said to myself - my voice quilted with the sadness of reality sealed by time, "in that house the passion was: i loved my daddy and my daddy loved my mother and never the twain shall meet."

Jimmie Gilliam
ED 14/15

This room is too

small.

You need another room
linked on
to this one.

A mirror on the wall
where the bed rests
would catch the window.

Dawn lights silver the river.
There is a person here
still sleepless
with the covers
folded around her.

The bed in the mirror
takes on the sheen of water.

The room moves into the doorway
which makes the room smaller.

Rachel Blau DuPlessis
ED 14/15

FRONTISPIECE FOR *HOUSES* ISSUE

UNDER THE ROOF

I am not sleeping and again the sun
is rising. Even the Wandering Jew
raises its arms, as if singing.
"Attack the enemy!" The Outer Limits
blares from the screen. An attack
of nerves, or is it habituation?
Sleeplessness-Sweden in winter-
when nights were clearer than days.

Last winter I moved into a building
in Brooklyn Heights, beside
the Lutheran's lone bell, opposite
the Presbyterian's off-key carillon.
The space was calm.
The building had stood a long time.
Across the street the brownstones
are painted numerous shades of red.

I came with a piano and the best
intentions. I came for the high
ceilings, the loft bed, the gas stove,
for the alcove, the recessed windows,
the archways, but hear footsteps
on the ceiling, voices in the bath,
eternities from one day to the next.

An alarm goes off. A voice asks:
- Do you know eternity?
- Do you know eternity?
- Do you know what time it is?
Below my windows they are speaking loud
and their accents are surprising on a Sunday
here in Brooklyn. At the tops of their lungs
German is what they are speaking, waking all
would-be late-sleepers within stone's throw
of the Deutsche-Evangelisch-Luther-Zions Kirche.

Half the church says '39, the other '87
and the signboard (Herzlich Wilkommen)
reads: Founded in 1855. The bell tolls.
- It must be eleven a.m.

The building has stood a long time.
Through the floors I feel the Hotel
Saint George battle the 7th Avenue Dragon.

Rika Lesser
ED 14/15

Waking Alone In Winter, 5 A.M.

Waking in you
sweet skin
in the only warm room in an empty house,
the first of the sun's light
streams to firelight
and the trees as they appear
are the queer masts of a great ship
coming in without wind.

Tam Lin Neville
ED 14/15

Waltz in "A" Minor

Sunday in the parlor.
The over-stuffed furniture.
She commands her son:
"Play me some Chopin"
He responds in "A" minor.
The sad waltz and a chalice
of Polish earth appear.
Chopin in a French Salon.
Mother and son in a Buffalo parlor.
And melody in the bass.

Time dissolves in three beats to the measure.
Majorca sunshine in East Side sleet.
Perfume of the Motherland
Rising from a spinet.
Blonde wood
Dark hair
White fingers

Swaying in time to the past.
Swaying in time to the past.

Philip Pawlowski
ED 14/15

At Stockman's

Three flights up, a sagging bunk,
Four plaster walls, one window -
Curtains yellowed from the smoke of cigarettes and pipes
(She always wipes the panes and the mirror clean
Before she shows the place, but wiping can't erase
The stains and smells that linger there) -
A peeling bureau, cold steel chair,
And, down the hall, a bath.
Twelve and a half a week, paid in advance -
She's learned that no one takes a chance
On anyone who'd seek a room
Above a cowboy bar. The view,
She thinks, is good enough since no one ever looks to see
The sagging wires, the weathered stair,
The sooty sparrows nesting there
Beneath the eaves. He pays, moves in, then leaves
Before the week is out, no doubt gone back
To open range or down to Norris where such rooms
Are only nine or ten. A feathered shadow
Darts down for a bit of string,
Then flutters back again.

Linda Sellers Peavy
ED 14/15

Crazy Ann

Her bedroom walls serenely sprout em
broidered flower gardens with for
get-me-nots and asters not to
mention bachelor buttons all cre
ated and perfected at the
funny farm

All glassy-eyed she worked the vibrant
colors through the whiteness till they
docilely accepted fate and
form within precluding lines and
when she did enough of them they
let her go

And now her garden thrives with shaded
flowers that can never get brown
edges or grow limp or drop their
petals one by one nor turn to
dust our crazy ann I think is
surely well

Susan Scott Thompson
ED 14/15

Outside the House

I lapse and you come back:
a jagged photograph, a flash-

The photograph is split
and I am on the other half.

Behind us,
the large wooden house
enormous willows at our sides,
bowing and shadowing our place.

We guard the entrance,
small and faceless.

I can not go in
but float   up and over
towards the field   that spreads
itself   into the sky,
black trees   bleed
against a screeching sun-

A morning, the field   plush green,
a sea   misplaced
the puppy runs through
separating waves   again and again.

Our voices come
from the house, at night
whispering
through the trees.

The puppy drinks   muddy water,
down   by the swamp
beyond the field.
I call, my belly mounding
to the sun.
He runs back   full-bellied,
belching
towards the house.

The sun is burning
a black hole in the sky,
the field is turning in thirst.
I hear you off in the distance.
You do not see.

Running in panic
through the field
I am a stomach-woman,
hiding among the trees,
kneeling and kneading the dirt,
laying down   among the wet roots.

The puppy is tied to a tree
by the house. Wailing   the ropes
too tight   cutting into his fur.

The field turns to gold.
I walk slow   through the tall
dryness.
I wait.

The willows are never naked,
the other trees, like skeletons
line the sky.

The willows shake,
the baby is brown
like the leaves   that have fallen.

The barren field   opens
beyond the swamp
to places
I have never seen.

Icicles hang from the house.
The dog   turns to stone,
is carted off   across the snow,
buried in the wood.

A circle of stones
mark his grave
The baby grows fur.

The field fades.

The house stands
vacant and echoing.

The dark clouds form,
the birds escape through the trees.

Elizabeth Quinlan
ED 14/15

Cleaning

Yes I have a broom the box
of Spic and Span's been opened
but matter doesn't like
to be contained as women
know our wombs twitch bellies
bulge fat grows around the hips
I'm careful
make sure I miss the corners
just coax it
into a mere pretense of
clean lines reassure us
this world is ours
well
this house
even so the wood groans at night
little hunks of plaster tear free and fall
there will be a revolt the walls
will swell bulge from the seams and burst the joints
the mortar crumble and the house cave in and spread
sprawl swallow the street where asphalt melts
and ferments and all the elements ooze
back to chaos

Rosmarie Waldrop
ED 14/15

Double Pillows

someone once said
the state of your bedroom
mirrors your lovelife

is that why
the lumps of clothes
like piles of old lovers

the dust in the corners
like old pain
hanging around

the wide open
bright spot of bed
like a hopeful vigil
that love will come
with double pillows
like love might stay

the antique patchquilt
where maybe love will
lie long enough
to grow old
and comfortable

ryki zuckerman
ED 14/15

Gloria

Gloria oils her
skin, her skin's
a honeycomb

spooning-up
icecream
at Foster's
Frosty Freeze

she watches the County Sheriff
patrol the blue seas &
the waves
stop & go

as the Sheriff figures out

& Gloria dreams she's
in a movie kissing the
County Sheriff on
a pineapple-sundae flight
to Hawaii

nibbling wistfully
through 15 birthdays she
swings
her giant legs
to & fro, but the Sheriff's
in lean cinerama

& Gloria's skin is a
honeycomb of
hexagonal wax

Sy Margaret Baldwin
ED 16

Sapolin Oyster White

(for Celia)

I pried the lid from the can of
paint, oyster white and thick
as hollandaise. And I stirred the paint,
making waves, almost spilling over the rim.

And I brushed the paint, brushing a
slurping sound, a
sound of heavy cream
like viscous love;
brushing walls and windows,
doors, baseboard, ceiling,
until my room was wet with it.

The next morning, sun lay
all over the walls,
lay like sun on beaches,
and it was like
waking in an oyster shell.

Ellen Bass
ED 16

Picking Pears

(for the woman in the poem)

Sunshine keeps you away from me.
Winter just won't come.
As long as the weather holds, you'll stay in Ontario
Picking pears.

At night you park the old truck
Somewhere outside Grimsby -
Hard little green pears for supper
With maybe a bottle of tequila
You bought for a day's pay -
You play your guitar by candlelight
And sleep on the metal floor these cold fall nights.

I ask you to come and stay with me
But you say that a day alone in a pear orchard
Is like some form of meditation
And you don't want to come down just yet.
While September lasts
I'll have to hold onto what I know of you:

If you get a pear with a rotten spot
In the middle of a pear orchard,
Throw it away.
If you get a pear with a rotten spot
In the middle of a city,
Save it and eat it in the dark.

Becky Birtha
ED 16

Suite M

The Plant
What causes the black spot
On my aluminum plant bought
In the dime-store? Whether rain or rot,
Insect or being in the sun too hot,
Its stalk grows firm but blight
Has struck its leaves and ends turn black
Curl up and feebly drop
Into the pot.
I search the block
For recipes and old maids eye
my little plot, to give advice,
What should I do? or buy?
To make it live. Take it inside
The wild man tells me, make it hide
From too hot wind, & run! Take it inside.

1. *The Top of the Stairs*
You stand at the top of the stairs.
I am asking you to come down, to forgive
your coldness. Come back down
the stairs. The prince has climbed
the tower, and in dreams
he should have claimed you.
Come back down the stairs. Passion
is precise. Suffering too.
Otherwise is no hope.

Make it soon, before the dead
go back to being dead: no one
to put up with you, no gestures left
to meaning, no room anywhere.

2. *Mount Snowdon*
You claim my bones as presence.
But the myth, the breathing space
around the real, that counts too.
I need to have you
as real as any picture book
Come back down the stairs. Let me have
daylight and mountain summer, you be
staff, good companion, cairn.
Wife's not family. But something else.

3. *Peat-Fire*
How to get inside another person's wants
that's always the problem.
And say you find out   what if all they want
is simple pure I want to be dead. To be
far away in a land with no shells
spotless. Doesn't anybody
stay in one place anymore. Ike said,
I only made two mistakes. Open the gates.
Bring commerce to the islands.
The land of heart's desire.

4. *Nice Weather but a Touch of Wind*
I hold onto the sides of the bed.
The snow is deep upon the ground.
The war is inside. Her outposts grow small and hard.
My mother, with my father, looked thus. And he was
  powerful
as a Harvard man with books. The war winds down.
My own makes its way, in folds and gathers.

Can you imagine the inside of the house next door.
Can you imagine what goes on in here.
So many rooms has a house but one roof. The war effort.

5. *Hound's Jaw*
The inside of the body too aches
To surround the other. The gut hangs
To spill out, mix like hot hands
With her stomach. Faces like drunk boats peer
On the barren reaches of the body
To claw and serve. Preserve us.
Sweet jelly roll.
All the genitals of the body proclaim.
My language hardens each day.
Hammers. Lungs swell. Peels.

6. *Under Hill*
The waters are sweet
The room we live in comfortable

9. *Seize*
If it were, if any word were
healing, it wd be
the cunts-cry, words
backlash, making
love, her unbearable

hot hearing, when youre locked
to it, a fucking mountain
to pull through

That flashlight
in you, that catastrophe, bearing
the hinged words
rise, her fuck coming at
you, loud and
strong, no questions, no more
blow and tell.

10. *Angel*
Not that quiet
is where its at, hardly that.
Instead, that the burbling, first instinct
the release
"unpremediated verse"
comes, a rampant
tongue. Her body is a cane
that breaks me, makes me suffer
all these years, in pain,
gladly, that she should stay
here. In this place where the only light
is what we make.
                                        She
bans it, refines it, discipline
to keep the edges firm, from running.
"Not that I dont feel." The politeness.
Arched back sings.

12. *Bride Bells*
Dont belabor me
"youre beautiful & you know it"
The waterglass on the bureau fills with morning
(Josephine's breast
molded, on the table, at the senator's right)

Nova Scotia
How long your lips drag mother
sea winds   gone companions
her meticulous white body
in the south   the highway
   low way   back-doorman
my DEW line

Marty Cohen
ED 16

JUNK

in each house
let's say conspicious
in the kitchen
a drawer
full of junk
extension cords, hammers, tacks, ribbed
rolling pin covers like old yellowed socks

domestic junk
that has no other place
which is dependable
which you can trust
reaching in & find
the razor blade scraper
under buttonhole attachment
consciousness involves
itself
all that disarray
of light switch plates
in 3 colors
brand new plastic
& scratched old brass
delving
under
paint stained putty knives
to rediscover
six leather covered buttons
the drive to reassert
to order
all
in neat arrangements
stacks & piles
coils & layers
repressed
the soul
in sympathy
speaks
let it be.

Joan E. Ford
ED 16

Joel Lipman
ED 24

ERLERNTER BERUF EINES VOGELS

1.

Gut geschlafen hat der Vogel im Vogelhaus. Er öffnet
die Augen, er freut sich auf etwas sehr Schönes, er
sagt:
Sehr schön sind Wasser und Köner, er frühstückt Wasser
und Körner. Das macht ihn fröhlich, er tanzt, er
holt
seinen Hut, hebt die Flügel und fliegt.

2.

Im Fliegen sagt er: Ich flieg über ein sehr schönes Land,
da unten frühstückt ein Mensch, ich werde ihm sagen:
Sehr schön ist Mensch, der ohne Pickelhaube frühstücken
kann, nicht minder ein Land, das den Menschen in jede
Vogelrichtung sprechen, schauen, frühstücken läßt.

3.

So, sagt der Vogel, das war recht einfach gesgat, aber es
musste gesagt sein, denn solche Klarstellung gehört ins
Kapitel der Freiheit, will sagen, zum erlernten Beruf
eines Vogels.

Gunter Werner Fuchs
ED 16

The Profession a Bird Is Educated Into

1.

He has had a good sleep, the bird in his aviary. He opens
his eyes, looks forward to a very beautiful event, he
says:
Water and seeds are very beautiful, he has a breakfast of
water
and seeds, it puts him in a good mood, he dances,
he gets
his hat, lifts his wings and flies.

2.

In flight he says: I am flying above a very beautiful
country,
down there is a man having breakfast, I will say to
him,
It is very beautiful for a man to have breakfast without his
spiked
helmet on, not to speak of a country which allows a
man to speak,
look, breakfast facing in any direction the birds fly.

3.

Well now, says the bird, that was easy enough to say but it
must also be said that such a clarification belongs
under
the heading "Freedom", that is to say, to the profession a
bird is
educated into.

Max Wickert *(translator)*
ED 16

Number 13

i took jesus
between the korean conflict
and the vietnam war
oh what tatoos that man had!

he was like a new green
i believed and believed
i was on a ferris wheel
that kept stopping at the top
i could see further than coney island

then his credit ran out
he got too sick to join a.a.

thursday
i called the greyhound bus terminal
is he in the men's room?
i got a recording
he is not
he is not
he is not

Terry Kennedy
ED 16

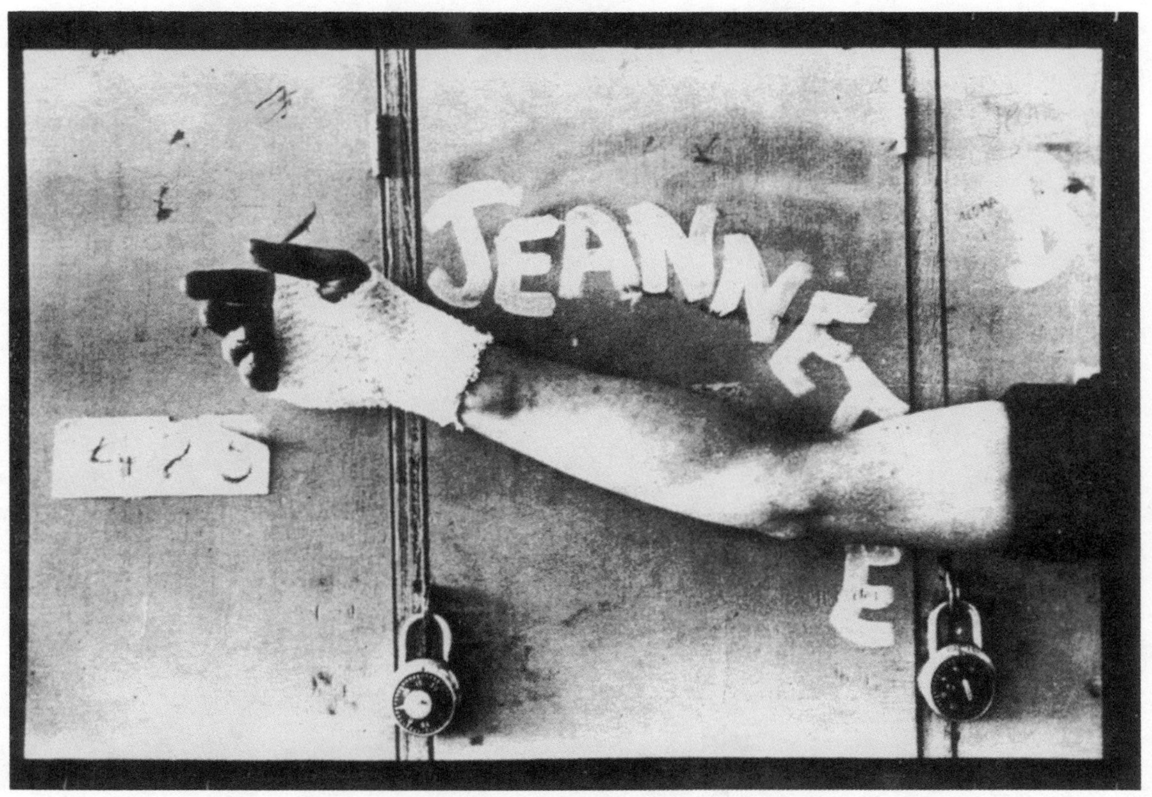

Debbie Jenks
ED 10/11

Your Manuscript We

are sorry the poems
we hardly publish
new poetry the most
exciting we've
seen for years
thank you for the
chance to we are
sorry know you
should have little
trouble we have
read with can not
pleasure publish
sorry unknown poets

lyn lifshin
ED 16

There! in the bright afternoon light
a woman stands by a birdcage shifting in shadow
She purses her lips in a flash of light
shaped like a great hand thrusting down
from the chimneys and roofs
clucking to her birds as she pushes food through bars
and her face is a face complete without revelation
in light the effortless color of asphodel.
She inhabits the full skin of her presence
an afternoon reality that holds the night at bay.
Her birds about her make a jungle clearing where the sun
filters onto her broad face and she changes with the
flickering
wings in flashes   flashes!
Her house in ruins around her sinks in a tangled garden;
she lingers in the light within
her wrinkled robe dabbled with red flowers
her dark hair streaming
talking to her birds in a low clear voice which rises
from the meshes of her serenity.
On the arm of silence she appears supreme in the moment
afternoon webbed in an orient of feathers
where her birds leap
like salmon
to the light.

Michele Murray
ED 16

The Prisoner

Determined to escape.
Every day
practising secrets in the barred place.
Building up strength. Examining the locks.
Slowly forging the papers, learning
to form the strange letters, grin
for the passport photo, add some hair,
alter the whole look of the eye, add
inches to your height, memorize
thousands of passwords. Learn to pass
casually by the guard, learn
every crevice of the cell.

After years of preparation
adolescence will disguise you all the way,
finally turn you into the grim
pitted face on the passport.
One day
THE GUARD DOZES BY THE GATE, YOU GO
as if invisible out into

the bronze metal body of the universe
unknown, free, and begin
sliding down her long greased
shining copper slopes, sliding,
sliding -

sliding -

Sharon Olds
ED 16

Family Portrait Just Before the Tragedy

Take a side of beef.
Hang it.
The hook be silver.
Cover it with honey.
Lower it
slowly
down to the coals.
Soon the skin will be
black and crisp.
Frost it with heavy white frosting,
butter and sugar,
frost the rib,
the flank,
the thigh,
cover it all. Candle it
with knitting needles.
Hang the needles
with hair, thread, tinsel, fur,
velvet, blood-clots, stand it up
there in the corner of the living room.
Bring the family round, Mother with her
blazing smile
shining like a beacon
SOS, bring on Father
smouldering like the bull ignited,
smiling around the firecracker
between his teeth, go get Sister in her
lost drown of petticoats,
her eyes painted on, the totem
head above her own a bear,
go get Brother from the firehouse,
curled asleep in the engine soaked
in gasoline,
his teddy dead,
line us up.
Father and Sister on that side,
Mother and Brother on that side and that's
me in the middle,
I am the elegant cow leg steeped
in elements. Snap us fast
before I do the next part
of my act - the only thing to do,
the only thing left to do.

Sharon Olds
ED 16

Death is Lying Down

Death is lying down
To sleep
And falling asleep.

The spirit says no
Sits upright, bolt.

It sets up camp
in the porch of the ear

It sets up machines
Tiny machines
Radios play
Old tunes   old tunes

Little cars
Circle streets
Crooked streets
Trying to park.

It says   no
I'm going further out.
The body waits for reports.

It hears rumors
The spirit was killed
By his crew.

It hears rumors
The sails were ripped
By a bird
With steel claws.

The body is discovered,
A continent, blue.

Balboa, Vespucci.

The spoilage begins.

Susan Fromberg Schaeffer
ED 16

Paula of the Wind and the Water

Caught between the devil and the deep blue
sea   riding the waves like riding
a man on his back   hooked onto that man
the sea frothing about her thighs   the devil
grinning   both horns shining above his forehead
his glowing eyes coming right out of the sky
at her   and she's laughing
as the swell takes her   as the wave rocks her
as her shoulders jerk with the unaccumtomed
pleasure of pure terror   because the devil
he's reaching out one longnailed finger
pointing it right out of the sky at her   drawing
a line of red along her shoulder   and when it's over
when the sea stops throbbing   she'll either be drowning
falling into a grey loss of temperature and air
that is her prison   her wedding gown
or she'll be captive of the air   streaming red
like ribbons of clouds at sunset from her torn body
as she shrinks from the unaccustomed terror of pleasure
the swarm of giggling devils   those agile masters
of the outer world   turning her freedom into
chaos   where she must make her way
or drown
caught between   caught
between   a long time falling   up down among the
elements
my friend Paula doing the 1970's doubletime rag-on dance
needing our prayers   needing our prayers
so she can learn how to ride the wind and the water.

Susan Fantl Spivak
ED 16

After Cleaning Ashes Of the Dresser I Sit Down to Read Artaud

"The sun seems to be staring.
But it stares as if it were *staring at*
the sun."
Antonin Artaud

After cleaning ashes off the dresser I
sit down to read Artaud
it is like looking in the mirror
his mouth,
in one photo,
bleeds with one of his own bones stuck
there like a cigarette conspicuously
chewed out
with that
RAZED-IN-HELL
'how-dare-you-crucify-me-when-I'm-
not-even-looking?' look
the self-conscious lips the overwhelming INVISIBILITY
Artaud in 1920
the lines in the cheeks RAZORSHARP
the icicle-scarred throat covered
carefully with a cadaverous scarf
ARTAUD THE ACTOR
Artaud of Boris Karloff eyes
eyes that rape heavens just by
looking up
ARTAUD who is wholeheartedly
hellish unthinkably so.
can I wipe the fire from your
face or must I wait for the ashes?
you who need no mirror to
look yourself in the eye.
you who defy mirrors
who defy photographs
you who perpetually spit at the sun
and then demand protection.

tell me who you are
& why there is moonblood on
your carefully folded fingers
tell me who you are
tell me who you are
& I will tell you how much
you escape!

Jayne Lyn Stahl
ED 16

The "Too-Bad-A-Woman-Doesn't-Have-Balls" Poem

So it was a biological faux pas.
The illustrious poetry board circled the two lines.
Five staid gentlemen, sitting slightly ahead on the
hard chairs, now that she had mentioned it, conscious
indeed of their damned balls.
        Freud had settled it once and for all; but here was
that lurking envy again (poor woman poet) sitting ahead
on the hard chairs, crowding the hour, coyly amused
by those wishful lines,
        "Too bad a woman doesn't have balls;
        her emasculation never shows."
hands cupped over crotch, possessing, pretending a bit,
and shifting a little in the hard chairs.

Linda Wagner
ED 16

Kastle Brill & Robin Willoughby
ED 17

Snake Lying in Leaves & Grass

I wanted to touch you
smooth looking skin lying so still
but all those childhood fears
taught to every desert girl

Your eye is dark and solemn
your jaw shut
you rest your head on a rock

I had my eyes closed for half an hour
Only you know
how long you've been watching

We watch each other now
After awhile you're bored
tongue the air and slide away

I wonder if all enemies turn out like this
long slender and silent
going their own way
through the grass.

Michele Connelly
ED 18

A Place in the Sun

I hadn't noticed
it was a rare sunlit Buffalo day

the weekend ice on Harlem Rd. drew
all the attention

but you were driving
and I was free
to mark the gravesites
to the right
offhandedly

then I saw light, light
that flowed and pulsed
from the sun's fingers
to the pointing stones
the glazed snow
in that frozen field gleamed
with a tenderness reserved for love
not death
between the ground and sky
the light returned
into itself
as if light could remove its shoes
to enter the Mirrored Room

this light - not that light
of physics in particles and waves
nor beams nor streams
this light bloomed, spilling
seed maturing instantly
it bloomed and spilled
and brew
a vast maw of light consuming
air, stone field and winter trees
and at last -
the right word comes
this was a light that breathed

Joan E. Ford
ED 18

2 Handed Shopping at St. Lukes

IN THE SECOND HAND STORE-HINTS

1. Look for the hidden item: diamonds disguised as buttons, the Magna Carta in a breast pocket.

2. Yes, you can buy sheets and underwear here.

3. Check the children's racks. Large sizes will often fit you.

4. Don't tell your friends to check the children's racks.

5. Smell the clothes before you buy them. Check for rips, stains, and messages from dead relatives.

6. These clothes have a history. Talk to them. Allow your children to ask them questions.

7. You are mixing with a stranger. You may be affected.

BRINGING THE CLOTHES HOME

1. Introduce your second hand clothes to your store bought items and leave them alone for awhile.

2. Your second hand clothes may chat about the pleasures of being steam ironed.

3. If this occurs, your permanent press garments will be jealous. Tell them you will wash them often.

4. When you wash the second hand items, do not hang them on the line to dry: they are modest.

5. The added years of your second hand clothes may tire you. Donate some of your well worn attire to a thrift shop to help alleviate this fatigue.

6. If you dream you are playing with dolls, be sure to examine their clothes. If they are the same as those you have given away, your apparel is in need of you.

7. The rags of your shirts will beat your window, claiming you from sleep so they can pluck your hair for thread.

8. Go to the mountains and find yucca with cilia the color of your hair. Weave a shawl and sleep with it over your head, and your clothes will find rest.

Sherri Lederman
ED 18

God, In Her Infinite Wisdom, Sends Crows

For weeks now god has been trying
to send messages with what is available.
Leaves, a thousand eyelids opening.
The iridescent scrawl of slugs.
God has been speaking
in the mundane waterfalls dripping off eaves,
the rare sunlight and the daily gift of mud.
And god has been especially
persistent about sending crows.

Suddenly black feathers appear at my feet.
Cr-aa-a-k audible above the thunk of an axe,
and the ringing phones at the office.
The visibility of crows with their
sunday strut on the fence,
their middle-of-the-week plump edge,
dark before the salt and foam of waves.
The self-satisfaction of crows in the wind
and on mowed lawns.
God guarantees crow-call on waking,
the only sure thing all day.

In the silence that lives in this house
and invites questions,
crows answer.
Leaning back in the steam of the tub,
I see wings, dark statements
in a grey sky.

When I am certain no one is about
I strike up conversations.

In simple terms:
I croon

And as god is my witness,
the crows listen.

Christina V. Pacosz
ED 18

To What Degree

The blackness of those robes
engulfs, enfolds
the paleness of
our certitudes.
What hall of
hallowed discipline
we came,
through solidified journals
and mouthing
papered wisdom.
We came through
those years
like an immortal sacrifice
to join the legions
in a sea
of allegoric hues.
We came
as guardians humbled
to this proud liturgy.
We came in honor
of the Flesh
made Word.

Mary Ann Schaefer
ED 18

When Does the Jacaranda Bloom?
(for my father)

I came to you,
wrapped in Florida's gentle sun.
It was Christmas,
and you were slower this time.

We walked slowly
around Florida's flat land
and hamburger stands,
eating when hungry,
sleeping when tired,
doing nothing, not even talking.
It wasn't necessary. Finally.

We have developed into silence,
where knowing is disclosed.
Days rolled into one another,
I never set my watch,
but told time by the shadows
creeping over your backyard.

When sun came to the camper,
it was ten o'clock.
By the time it reached
for the side of the house,
it was noon.

We sat quietly and did nothing
whole days in a row.
I yielded to sleep for long hours,
or reading reading rocking rocking
reading.

From your porch,
we watched the jungle
take over like a picture show.
Vines smothered trees,
while other plants with tentacles
and big green fan leaves
reached for ground to start anew.

I'll take some home, I said.
They will not grow in snow, you said.
We left it at that.
When does the Jacaranda bloom? I said.
Later, you said, later.

I'm lonesome these days, you said.
Me too, I said.
The world has grown up around me,
you said, and I never knew you -
you never knew me.
It is better that way, I said.

We exchanged disappointments,
listed them and shared remorse,
then slipped into the sun of Tampa Bay,
kneading the sand between our toes.
We laughed as the dog
licked a bald man's head
as he lay on his belly in the sand.

We parted in airport chaos,
not even a full-bodied hug,
only desperate kisses on quick lips.
I set my watch. Finally.
A tear pale-purpled down your cheek.

I'll come again in summer, I said,
when the Jacaranda blooms.
When *does* the Jacaranda bloom?
I called back.
Later, you answered, later.

Joy Walsh
ED 18

Florida Roots

for Sandra Mae

She follows her latest husband's
jobs and non-jobs
and ideas of jobs,
each time wringing
chapped hands over
forgotten pots and
pillowcases,
even rags - hard to come by
in a new house,
a bare apartment.

Each time
she plants a garden "down back,"
hoeing and weeding,
watering,
shooing off birds
from the sanctuary.

The rent comes due -
another move.
Behind stretch perspectives
of hoed rows,
converging at the horizon.

At her heels spring
green shoots.
On the horizon -
waving tassels
and swollen vines.

Ann Fox Chandonnet
ED 19/20

Linda

that longing
never forget it but I remember
an outlaw

you're all gussied up yearning for
a wedding gown
but we grew up another era
together
we stayed up
together
for days and nights sparking
together
laughter in your eyes.

now the end is near
you may not don't
see me again ever
since you let that magic die
took up his offer

K.S. Ernst
ED 19/20

This evening
in a college bar
eighth day of Christmas   you
drink bourbon straight   tell
  stories of the new love

for my comfort

I'll have another cream liqueur   you
love me say if
only I had told you
of the other men   perhaps

but now...

Beyond your right ear
snow is falling quiet
in and out of me the
snow is falling
like clean tears

which other men?

you'll miss me
when you go to momma's   call
from Pittsburgh
from Atlanta
Birmingham   you'll
call from bars in Tuscaloosa
collect
at 3 a.m.   and put
your buddy Roddy from Natchez on
the pay phone
at the Wicked Chicken   boy
he'd like to meet me
when he comes to Cleveland

Other men.

Outside   snow falls ungreening me

I'll have another cream liqueur   and I suppose
love other men and Roddy   if I ever
get to Natchez
                                        or Cleveland.

Patricia Donovan
ED 19/20

How Much Longer

How much longer
will hearing your name
  burn my face
  like a slap;
  pinch off my breath
  like a thumb
  at my throat;
  make me stop and turn
  like a tap
  on my shoulder.

How much longer
will hearing your name
  suspend the neat
  arrangement of my life;
  shove me sharply
  into that awful hesitation

  where I gather in
  your absence.

Judith Geer
ED 19/20

Love Poem at End of Summer

Like death, you never said when you were coming.
Yet without the threat of death or you
my blood would be wineless and these leaves simply red.
What has happened coincides like a cliche with the
seasons.
Even in that dry white August
I heard the streams running
while waiting for September like sun setting.
Now in Fall fire, knowing that you are going,
that smaller death about to make its visit,
I sit brave as old winter people in frame cottages
warming themselves with the timeless optimism of
knowing
that every year after ambushing us in that green sensuality
the branches bare themselves to surprise us
by revealing the enormous protective forms of mountains.

Iris Litt
ED 19/20

Drunk in the Snow

Long rows of bare hickory trees
and a cold sun in February no one
could consider praising, clouds moving apart
the way you must be moving by now
into this hard ground.
In the morning I walked out and thought
about your weak heart, the cast-iron statue
of the Indian Maiden at the center of the town park
that you tried to make love to, drunk
in the snow coming back from Boney's Bar.
You climbed her greening legs
and sang her all your favorite songs,
convinced that no woman could remain all metal or stone.
Twenty feet in the air you looked lonely,
loose-lipped, believing in the days and nights,
the pigeons flapping around your head and shoulders,
cold hand raised against the sun,
staying there longer
than an hour, whispering in her ear.

From dream to dream you gave yourself
until you found another dream to live in. I am
alone without you under this graying sky,
but happy, almost dancing again
to your harmonica the way we danced
on the cracked linoleum, and I find myself
here humming in the snow, kicking dead leaves off
your stone, amazed at this gift of living and dying.

Len Roberts
ED 19/20

15th Anniversary

the 15th anniversary is crystal because
it shatters so easily   15 years gone
into it, a new adolescence approaching
you want to do it all over again before
it's too late but you are afraid in the
mirror and your teeth are bad   you
see the future before you like a glass
staircase   you do not want what is
to continue, you do not want to accept
what will be   your children throw
stones at your image, your future is
not theirs anymore   you drink too
much, smoke too much, lose weight
gain weight, examine yourself in
the mirror   frozen, you make no
move, wait for the last stone to
decide   the 15th anniversary is
crystal because it shatters so easily

Helen Ruggieri
ED 19/20

After Being Rejected by Your First Lover

You will notice
the Italian olive tree,
its roots spreading into the lawn,
its raised bark frozen
in curling tear drops.

Later you will remember
the hot Florentine summer
you met him;
even the statue
of the Virgin
had breasts and thighs
under her
marble gown.

Nancy Sarah Schoellkopf
ED 19/20

Kiss Me Goodnight

& if you come to me
In the morning
I'll meet you at the front door
With two luminous snifters
Half-filled with topaz moondrops
From Armagnac

& if you come to me
At midday
I'll be drying my hair in the sun
You'll turn the nozzle
Of the blower
As I settle my head in your lap

& if you come to me
In the afternoon
I'll be reading Carlos Baker's
Biography of Hemingway
I'll be laughing, crying
& trying to take a nap

& if you come to me
at 6 PM
I'll offer you breast of pigeon
For dinner
Sauteed with garlic, rosemary
& fresh wild mushrooms

& if you come to me
In the evening
I'll be wearing my favorite T-shirt
Dingy yellow
With a faded black logo: "Kiss me
Goodnight"

& if you come to me
At midnight
I'll be sleeping peacefully
In the arms of another stranger
Please shut the front door tightly
Love, before you walk away

Joanne Seltzer
ED 19/20

The Divorce

I could
turn your picture
to the wall. But
that would be too close
to irony
we spent the last yr. sleeping
with our backs
facing
each other.

Conversations pregnant
with senile pauses
we had forgotten
how to talk
to each other; language
had deteriorated to neanderthal facial
grimaces.

I stared at
fly strips disengaging
from the ceiling with the downward
parabolic weight of the flies. They
are still there

you always took the trash out.

We sit
opposed
two beer glasses frosted I
see your hair moving
toward its winter camouflage. You talk
about loneliness
you were never one for laundry
doing
your own socks I smell
your death.

Conciere Taylor
ED 19/20

Female Admitting

what time is it?
what day is this?

did i actually drown the children?

memory has not been kind to me
here

oh - the house was saved you say
yes, i wanted to burn it down
to the ground yes i remember wanting
to do that
no i am not sorry doctor

what day is this?

where is my husband?   I will be good
call my mother please and daddy too
do you have a cigarette   I will return the matches,
please

you ask such personal questions, doctor
I don't remember masturbation, flirtation,
menstruation, fornication
orgasm?
orgasm's a man's question
no I don't remember any and my husband
considerately
did not ask

may i go now please?
NO DOCTOR I AM NOT ANGRY I NEVER GET ANGRY
I have always been nice and good like mother told me
no she never touched me
mommy and daddy touched each other
daddy was very quiet mostly but
i do remember his soft hands on my breasts, his
mouth between my legs, yes i am ashamed very ashamed
i am sure it was my fault   no i am not angry at him
i am not angry at anyone please don't tell mommy
we never talked about these things

may i go now doctor, please
no more questions may i have another cigarette, I'll
return the matches, please
Of course i put the girls
in the bathtub
that's where you drown things and
yes i called the fire department
isn't that the proper thing to do

will i be getting more Thorazine doctor
or Stellazine soon
dinner will be ready soon
are the girls ready for dinner
what funeral arrangements
my husband is the organizer
please talk to my husband about those things

what day is this?

are you going so soon doctor
oh - i have so much more to tell you
please, more questions, please
don't go now

i am just starting to feel good with you
what is that you are saying, you're being
transferred to another hospital
i'll be seeing doctor Hernandez? Why can't I
have you
Why can't I have a woman doctor I want a woman
doctor No I don't want to leave now doctor
all right I'll get out and fuck you
go ahead and leave me **YOU GET OUT**
I hate talking to you anyway

No doctor I am not angry please stay
i'll be good
where is mommy where is daddy
may i walk in the yard now
are the girls all right
no i am not angry doctor
thank you and
have a nice day

Geri Grossman
ED 21

playback

a moment slips off the shelf
and rattles around;
all the dominoes fall down;
the scenario is stuck on rerun;
no incision necessary to survey the contents
just

peel back the scalp, spilling:
unravelled reels of frenzied film
dream entangled with breath
gyroscopes spiralling laughter
elsewhere soundless moving mouths

peel back the cranium, emptying
stolen shadows, silent screams,
greedy thalamus gorges on
whispers which shiver the tiny cilia
on the nape of the neck

a blue electric moan
edged with pale phosphorous
crackles across the retina.

ryki zuckerman
ED 21

Terry Gross & Judy Treible
ED 3

They Are Riding In A Car

They are riding in a car. They are satisfied because finally it is unquestionable. They will all ride together and will turn their faces in the same direction. Back down the hill in the dense green foliage. The dark one will drive. She knows the way. She has always known the way and now will establish
the understanding. The child goes without complaint, trusting. And the woman beside her, with the white wrinkles and the
piercing blue eyes, listens to the irrelevant worry, the one about going the wrong way, that chatters on her shoulder, as if it were the last bird singing in the twilight that draws her down. They're perfect together, each one knows it. And ride silently toward their destination on the enthralling road.

Catherine Jackson Is Seated At The Harp

Catherine Jackson is seated at the harp. With frizzy gray hair, dangling earrings and her long powdered nose. Long bare arms, gathered satiny skirt with hand-painted flowers spread over her knees. *My mother said I'd never amount to a hill of beans.* Her strong callused fingers pressing into the strings. Then swishing out the door, her high laugh a glissande, she lifts her foot in the elevated red leather shoe, into her yellow jeep and disappears over the hill. Her handwriting swirls gaily over the page: *You can do whatever you want.*

Janine Canan
ED 22

Vicarious Experience

I'm behind you all the way, blond boy.
My hands are under your denim jacket,
clutching the folds of skin on your belly
where the large buckle cuts in.
I put my face to your long grass hair
getting to know your windy smells -
I twitch like a marmot in the brush.
You think I'm the worn old lady in the
car behind on the Big Sur Road.
You passed me and glanced with contempt
at my ruined face. But you're wrong,
boy, you're wrong. I'm flying with you.
I'm here as you force your knarled machine
holding it with bony knees legs while
we climb and swoop on our deadly trail.
I reach around, a friendly lecher, and pull
the coarsened hair below your cut-off pants.
The waves make kissing sounds and wait,
wait as you miss your curve and then
you're really flying boy, out into
the hideous glare...I'm with you there,
Flying Boy, I'm with you all the way.

Sally A. Fiedler
ED 22

The Bird Killer

bounced another off the
windshield this hot morning
on my way to work
a black one/flying low and
trying to swoop across the road
wings heavy with moisture

I saw it smash against the
pavement in my rear-view
mirror as I eased off the
brake/shuddering//slammed my
foot on the accelerator for
a fast getaway

last year it was worse/the car
sought them out/thudding them
against its grill and hood
the corner of the roof beside my
head///makes no distinction
between sparrows and
snowy owls

now she prowls the roads
sure of her skill/looking for
bigger game

Bonnie Johnson
ED 22

My father
watched the Indy
on t.v.
He said:
Women don't drive
in it because
they can't handle
all that power.
I said:
Women don't drive
in it because
they wouldn't waste
all that power
going in circles

Julie Kay
ED 22

Driving for Yellow Cab

it pretends to be a place:
coffin, flowerpot
a yellow carapace
the price of money
keeps going up

no change
"I've been waiting half an hour.
I thought
the Hell with her!
I'm going to finish my beer!
But then, I thought you might
leave without me."

the gentleman who doesn't tip, the lady
hurrying, the gambler who pays extra
if I catch his bus
to the track
the black lady gogo dancer
fringed on Sunday
the woman with seven kids
and six bags of laundry

I sit in front of the Greyhound station
with three Independents ahead of me
cruise the supermarket pickup lanes, hungry
high-flagging when I can
mostly frustrated

pretends to be a home, a place, sitting
waiting for the dispatcher
number different every day
car different, the same black grit
on my hands, slamming and opening doors
counting out change
"Every driver an escort."
sometimes so busy I can't
raise the dispatcher, ducking in
between other drivers' transmissions
"25." "25." until the dispatcher yells

shut up so he can give an order
or waiting at the stands to move
watch ticking, meter silent
sometimes for hours
trying to read, distracted
by the lost time
"Hey 38. You asleep?"

the meter clicks minutes, miles
a pleasant hour in the snow
taking an old man shopping
$7 looking for wedding shoes
on Sunday afternoon in Spring
the airline pilot asks me where the action is

I don't mind waiting
with the meter running
I can't back up a oneway street
I smile at old ladies who assure me
they're only going a little way
when I've waited half an hour for the call
now I'm 7th on the list again
five old ladies, five one-dollar fares
for church on Easter morning
But Easter's a good day
no one's on the street
the price of everything

"Is that clear, 17?"
"Clear."
drunk men who always want to sit
up front, always make time
never tip
the pretty woman, drunk and sad
her fiftieth birthday, she says
as I help her around to her back door

bad brakes, ice under the wheels
a man shouts
"I ain't going with no
woman driver!"

it pretends to be a time machine
a species, a yellow family
Humboldt, Guilford Street
the Chippewa red-light district, the far West side
the guy in the car stage-whispers
"She doesn't wanna go with you,
cause she's a Lezzie."
Hari Krishnas, ten in the back seat
singing out the windows

try to hustle me for the fare
it's my yoga: sit in the sun
at the cabstand, enjoy the day
forget you're losing money
a practice of love
with a knocking engine and no seatbelts
to stop resenting
a buck-fifty fare with no tip
I forget
how long I have been
moving, looking for the street
the number, the street
check the sheet: 5 minutes
gluing the corners of the town together
"You're number 5 at the loop, 41."
the price of nothing, my time

Judith Kerman
ED 22

Driving Across the Texas Night

my only thought was flight
as though the house were flame
the night I placed
the sleeping children
four logs
in the old station wagon
(the night he tied me to the bed)

then there was no thought
of the nights we heated
the cold room with our bodies
two logs
coddling the fire between
our limbs

I dropped the diamond ring
in an oil can
the first station
I stopped for gas

Patti Renner-Tana
ED 22

Feu D'Artifice

No names for any of this.
Naming not the purpose.
Anyway there is the language problem.
List all the verbs, they still remain
infinitive   conditional
not finite to our touch -
until the lights go on
(the feu d'artifice of Bastille Day)
and with a rush room 518
transforms to flames
the balcony ablaze
and we go over, over
our own names
we mispronounce or don't
pronounce at all.
It matters little.
Brighten. Brighter. Bright.
Your name, Gerard, exploding
in the night.

Ansie Baird
ED 23

Love Is When One Frees
for Cass on her birthday, 1982

By completing the other's life without
deviating in the least from his/her
own life which is reciprocally
allowed to be itself so that it
can complement the other's,
and by so doing the snares of
one are untied by the other while
neither need to do anything but be
present in their actual life
which is always superior to
the other's fate, thus to trust
becomes the principle not only of
relation but the living dead who
otherwise prey on us for rest.

Jack Clarke
ED 23

Yes

i could have you love me
like this like caramel melting
so easily i could have the star
in black sapphire gleaming
your eyes when you love me
and never stop looking
your eyes see if i love you
like roses in ferns
so perfectly in place
like the hairs on the edge of my hair
in an ideal order of their own
fall into place
like snow fitting neatly
like you lay on the spaces
& your fingers glide where it's smooth
& your tongue glides where it's sweet
& the words fall into flawless music as my name
i could have you love me
like this for many days
like the time it takes for leaves
to brighten and fall til they all
have made a lush cover i could
like caramel melting so easily/yes.

Thulani Davis
ED 23

Kastle Brill

You showed me
a photo of yourself
revealing
only a portion

Tough eyes
a characteristic
thrust of the head
That don't mess
with me look

But another
caught you
softer and smiling

Still another pose
reflected only in
your lover's eyes
A face
full of wildness
as a mare
galloping across
an open field
Ecstatic brilliant eyes
dazzled on
the verge of climax

Dennis Maloney
ED 23

Thor
you say

soft spoon
no thunder

stick and cup I

stroke the slope of
shallow bowl
the
swelling softness
of your
underside

my thumb

has found a
worry stone
to slide against again
again

your name:

  a spoon a

  spoon

the tongue would fit.

one part for
grasping.

this,
the oval smoothness
that will part the lips:

a gift.

Pat Donovan
ED 23

Carla's Poem

Long after dinner
we are still at the table
dishes not quite cleared
time full and rich,
suspended
as it is when saints
raise a hand to speak
or angels bring news of wonders.
The baby begins to kick and move
inside my daughter.
I bring my face hard up
to the wall of her womb,
I cup my hands,
and loud with love I call:
    Hello, hello
    I am your grandmother,
    I am waiting for you,
    hello, hello.
No answer but my daughter's laughter
over my head
and the shrill light of a flashbulb
- a family picture of grandmother
talking to the baby.

Olga Mendell
ED 23

Down

We chew and chew on each other's
spicy flesh, a curry, a potroast
and do not spit the other out.

I stood in the sugar cane
near Cien Fuegos and bit on the green
fibrous stem and the sweetness flowed.

Come let us raise our tent of skin.
Let me wrap you in the night of my hair
so our legs climb each other like peavines.

The tiger lily is open on the freckled hour.
Bite into its ruddiness, a peach
splitting with ripeness and juice.

We plunge into each other as into a pool
that closes over our heads. We float
suspended in liquid velvet.

The light comes from behind the eyes,
red, soft, thick as blood, ancient as sleep.
We build each other with our hands.

That is where flesh is translucent as water.
That is where flesh shines with its own light.
That is where flesh ripples as you walk

through it like fog and it closes around you.
That is where boundaries fail and wink out.
Flesh dreams down to rock and up to fire.

Here ego dissolves, a slug in vinegar,
although its loud demands will come back
like a bounced check as soon as we rise.

But this dim red place that waits at the pit
of the pool is real as the bone in the flesh
and there we make love as you make a table

where the blood roars like an ocean in the ears
remembering its source, and we remember
how we are bound and body of each other.

Marge Piercy
ED 23

Massaging the Perineum

Once, seven years ago, a touch
like this would make us faint,
all blood rushing to our sex,
and sometime late the next afternoon
we would sit patiently brushing
knots out of each other's hair.
It's different now.

I lie back against pillows,
eating rice pudding from a plastic cup,
scraping its bottom for the cream
and cinnamon,
while you dip fingers in olive oil
and slide them in a horseshoe pattern
around my perineum, stretching out
a smooth passage for the child to come.
It's a chore.

Seven years ago we didn't know the word
"perineum." We didn't use the words
we did know often.
I said then that the sight of you
slinking naked up the stairs
for me to follow
left me dumb.
Today that same dance
would be danced for laughs -
you a parody of Pan,
I a grotesque nymph,
lumbering up the stairs after you.

Yet, this morning, in the bathroom,
my breath caught for the thousandth time
watching you from behind.
You pulled down your tee-shirt
with something like real modesty
to prevent my staring,
holding my eyes with yours in the mirror
while you brushed your teeth.

And tonight, though we oil and stretch, spoon and yawn,
familiar with the word for the tissues between
and the feel of them,
familiar with so much
and far from fainting,
we are built somehow to forget it all
and mime the old dances once again like two goats
who have surprised each other on a craggy peak.

Sherry Robbins
ED 23

The Red Cat

Like the red cat,
Brought home as a kitten,
Under a boy's warm coat,
I take my pain
Under a chair somewhere,
Perhaps to die of it,
For truly, like the animals,
Who have far more sense
About things like this,
We live entirely in our own skin.

You are not there
When I need you most.
Sometimes I think of you as a ghost.
Some myth or fiction I conjured out of need.
Our need for fictions is strong
In this world of inventions.

So, like the red cat,
Who hid under a boy's bed,
I take my pain
Out in a field somewhere
To lick my wounds
Or die of them.
There is a certain dignity
In this animal procedure.
It is not sad,
Only facticity.

Your life is full
Without me.
I am but an aside,
Outside of everyday reality,
Like taking out the garbage,
Or putting the groceries away.
I am the myth of your invention.
I have allowed you this.
Therefore the fault is mine.
Not yours.

So, like the red cat
Who licked the face of a boy
Then crawled under an old shed
Away from touch of others -
To heal or die,
With an economy
That is somehow compelling,
I move again
Into my own skin.

Joy Walsh
ED 23

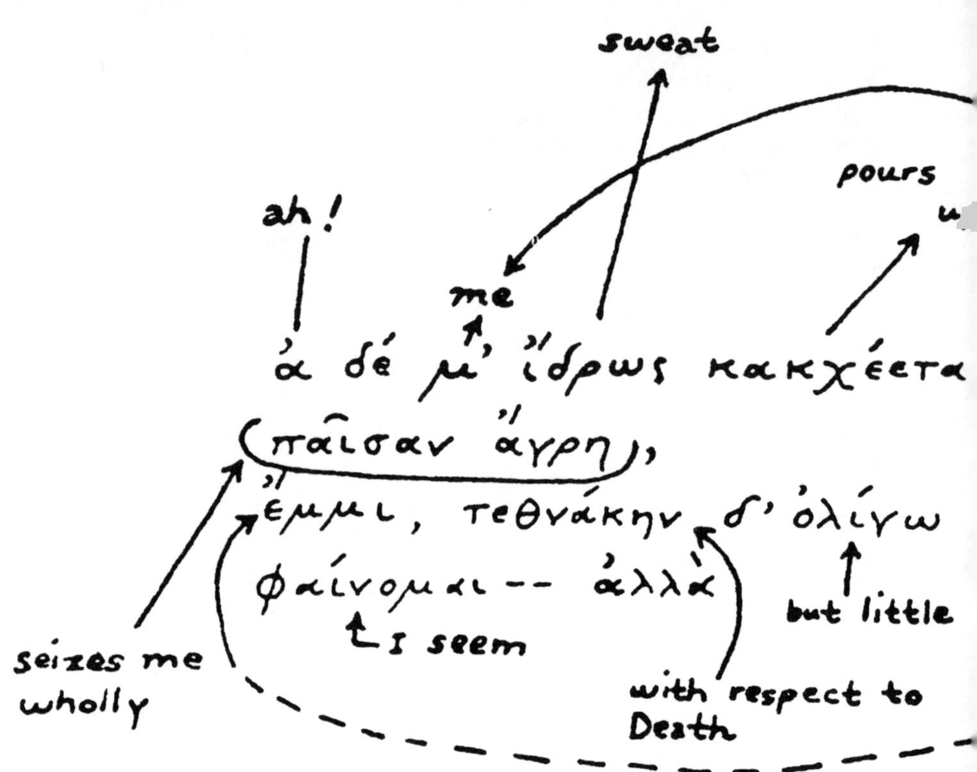

Equal to the gods
is the man who sits
in front of you leaning closely
and hears you sweetly speaking
and the lust-licking laughter
of your mouth, oh it makes my
heart beat in flutters!

When I look at you
Brochea, not a part of my
voice comes out,
but my tongue breaks,
and right away
a delicate fire runs just beneath
my skin,

I see dizzy nothing,
my ears ring with noise,
the sweat runs down
upon me, and a trembling
that I can not stop
seizes me limb and loin,
o I am greener than grass, and
death seems so near....

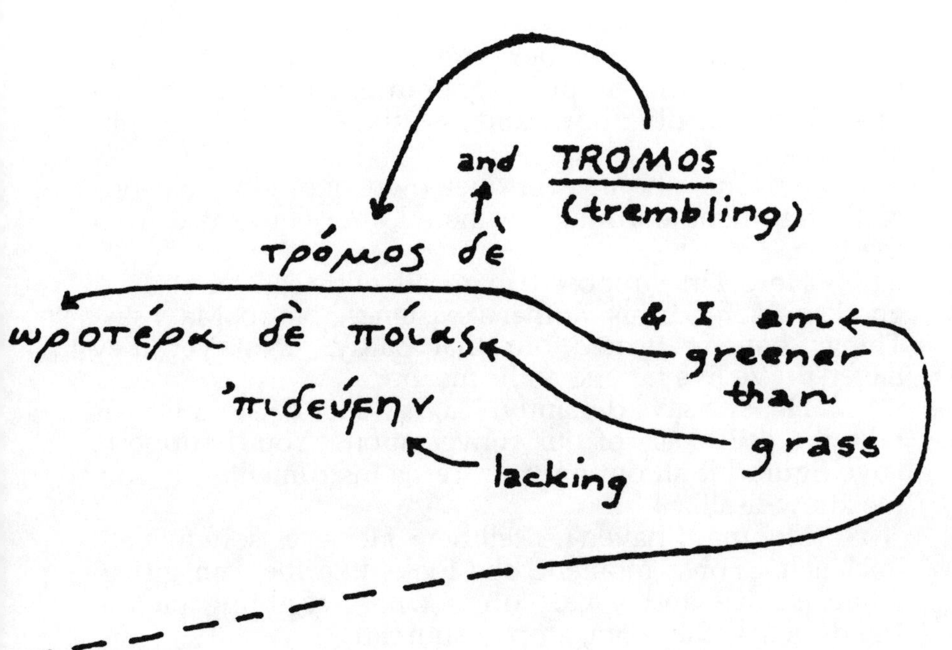

ON THE QUESTION OF BODY TONES

To

topos / typos / tropos

be added

tromos

The Trembling
that Sappho felt
at the sight of
Brochea

Ed Sanders
ED 23

Blue Baby

I didn't ask to be born, my mother says. It was an accident. A case of pure ignorance. Who can tell a seventeen-year-old boy and a sixteen-year old girl anything?

No one, she answers her own question. No one could tell them anything. So here I am. Unwanted from the start.

Here I'm supposed to recoil with contrariety. A good son defends his mother's existence. No so, Ma, I say. Things haven't turned out that badly. Not yet they haven't. We live far above the mean.

Ha, she says defiantly, Ha, ha. Her boisterous eyes rake the dull coals of our conversation. You, I suppose, have figured it all out on your Texas Instrument. My son, the know-it-all.

No, ma, I haven't, I tell her. Her eyes soften, teeth unclench. For a moment, she looks like the thin girl in white pumps and a pale dress whose wedding picture stands across the room, atop the bureau.

I dropped the damn thing last week, I tell her. I think it's ruined. All it does now is spit out zeros. Besides, you know what I meant. I was speaking qualitatively.

You were generalizing, she says. You were pretending to be disinterested. But you're not, she smiles. Like it or not, you're a part of this story. You're one of its consequences.

There was a time in my mother's life when she lived almost totally without men. During the War years, she says, a girl could grow up at a more leisurely pace. All the men were away. Life was less of a circus. Little did we know, she sighs, that they were fighting over us.

The kettle boils. She moves to turn it off. What'll it be, she asks. Coffee excites your nerves, and tea stains your teeth.

Coffee; black, no sugar, I recite, as if she has forgotten my preferences. As if I were not so much her son as someone else's. As if God had penciled my name onto his scorecard: Designated son.

So what's the matter with men, I ask her. Aren't we useful to have around? Sometimes even necessary?

No doubt, she says. Especially the latter. "Necessary," I always liked that word. It takes all the pain out of choosing.

She pours boiling water into my cup slowly. Gives it six quick stirs with a teaspoon. I watch her arms move. Her breasts. Her pre-arthritic wrists.

No, men are fine. Good company, some of them. The world as far as they know it, is theirs. Yours, I should say, she corrects herself. My sons have grown. Even though they're still my sons, they've now grown into....men.

When I was younger, my mother says, I sometimes felt the need to be alone. To just go off somewhere for a week or a month. Pack a suitcase, that's all. Not tell anyone when or where.

She looks away for a moment, embarrassed. Who knows what she might confess to if she continues on in this vein. It's raining tonight. Hard. In our silence, we hear its soft crescendo on the roof, its cleansing surge through the gutters.

Of course, there are certain things you trade off in life, she resumes. What kind of mother would leave her kids, hop aboard a Greyhound? In time, it even affects your dreams. Deaths and marriages, you dream, never love. And on certain cold nights, you dream of being a girl again.

"Your father and I...," my mother used to begin when the time came for passing down judgments. Your father and I have decided to raise your allowance to a quarter. Your father and I think that you should spend more time on your studies. Later, my brother and I would learn that Dad was never in on any of these "decisions." He merely assented to them. Lent his firm hand and his silent brown eyes to their sovereignty.

It was not as if he did not have opinions. He had as many as the next guy. But that was all they were: opinions. My mother's word was law.

One Sunday afternoon when I was six, my mother told me about the End of the World. The End of the World, she said, would come about by Fire. It would come by Fire because God had used Water once already, with mixed results, and did not want anyone down here on earth to think that he was just a one-trick deity.

Fire will be quicker, she warned. None of that forty days and forty nights business. Besides, He knows all about the Queen Mary.

I think that the purpose of her tale was to caution me against playing with matches, a pack of which had been found in my trouser pockets the previous wash-day. But it was the incidental effect of her story that she could not control. Resurrections was a tall order, even for six-year-old, to swallow. But death - Dad's death, and her's - could be imagined.

I was nineteen-years-old before I brought a girl home to meet my mother. She was a doe-eyed brunette named Paula. Ten months later, she would marry a square-jawed mechanic named Frank. But that night, I brought her home to meet my mother - who had hot water ready on the stove, and the chairs in the parlour arranged in a semi-circle.

Call your dad, she said. He's in the garden. In fact, she knew him to be in the basement. So did I. But out to the garden I went.

So, my mother began, as Paula recounted to me later. So, you have designs on my son, she said. What makes you think you're good enough for him? Paula put out her cigarette, looked out the window.

Let me tell you something, she continued, the boy's no angel. Even as a baby, he loved his titty. If I were you, I'd be careful. Use some kind of protection. Don't count on him, he thinks he's Kierkegaard or something. A spirit. She brushed up against Paula's shoulder, pouring coffee, stirring.

You're not a bad-looker, my mother said, smiling broadly now. You should get some clothes that fit you. Never mind what the boys like. They're all the same until they turn fifty and their backs go bad. Half their lives they spend thinking with their glands.

When she was born, my mother weighed barely four pounds. Within a week, she had contracted pneumonia. The doctor who had delivered her shook his head and rode off. I am only a layman, he said, you need a priest.

The baby was slowly choking. Its face turned from a translucent white to a kind of muted blue. The color of sick potatoes. The color of the moist towellettes they hand you in airplanes.

Undaunted, my great-grandmother Gehrig applied her own treatment. She had heard, from the women folk of the town, of the rare curative powers of dry heat and chicken fat. She placed the baby girl in a roasting pan and coated her febrile chest with a thick layer of the grease that had congealed atop the previous day's soup. She set the pan and baby into her oven above the lowest possible flame. Left the oven door open for circulation

For two weeks, she and her railroader-husband and their thirteen children kept vigil. For two weeks, they ate chicken. Chicken stew. Chicken soup. On Saint Joseph's Day, the fever broke. The baby wailed, screamed, giggled.

Another one saved, my great-grandmother said to her railroader-husband. How will we feed her?

You'll never find a woman, my mother tells me, as long as you insist on resorting to theatrics. You can get someone's attention that way, but you'll never hold it. Forget the hearts and flowers stuff. It's not an easy business, loving someone, she says. You shouldn't pretend that it's all like in the movies.

My mother knows all about the movies. She learned to speak English by attending afternoon matinees on the advice of her night-school teacher at the International Institute. Spencer Tracey, she would watch, and Katharine Hepburn. Doris Day and Donald O'Connor. She understood just a fraction of what was said. But enough, she tells me now, to understand the genre. More than enough.

She hasn't been to see a film since "The Sound of Music." Television doesn't count, she says. The screen's too small. She had wanted to see "Last Tango in Paris," which starred Marlon Brando, and sounded like a lovely romance, until she read otherwise.

And just to think, she muses, they say he now weighs three hundred pounds.

If you are going to be a writer, my mother tells me, you should at least not write lies. Even if it's in your nature, you should resist it. Give your characters a decent chance. People aren't as stupid or mean-spirited as you would have them. Nor are their lives as dismal and empty. If you'd only get out a bit more, you'd see that. That Thomas Hobbes fellow you're forever quoting probably never raised his head out of the muck.

My mother is dressing to see her doctor. Blue slacks, she chooses, and a fresh white blouse. High blood-pressure. It will probably kill me someday, she says cheerfully, but there's no timetable. That's the good news, she says. So many ways to die, but only one way to live.

Dad is out running errands. She borrows my car. Your father and I, she begins, can take care of each other. She seems distracted now, almost nervous.

But it's nice of you boys to help.

I touch her wrist as she starts the car and backs it gently out of the driveway. Once in the street, she gives me a thumbs-up signal and waves.

I watch her drive off in my little red sedan until she is just a punctuation mark in the mid-afternoon haze. Tomorrow the haze will lift, but I won't be here to see it. There's a wedding at noon in the North Chapel, and I have promised to be there.

R.D. Pohl
ED 23

The Dreamtime

I

dreamtime connects
families clans couples
cultlodge guilds of workers in the same
material a mystery iron
or wood

II

  feminine
the souls always female man
souls woman souls shes meet in
the dreamtime

Sam Abrams
ED 24

Workshop of the Rose

Here in my workshop I have emptied
every beakerful of description, made
leaden tongue turn gold for the asking,
asked what color you would like.

The answer is in your poetry: patent
red-leather petals on a spiked stem
standing lewd in a virgin-white vase
        before your doorstep.

            Traditional love
is most deadly, most difficult.
You don't know the American Beauty
I had to bleed to get just that shade.

Michael Alexander
ED 24

HE

MESSIAH HE

HE HE
HE HE HE
HE HE HE
HE HE
HE HE
HE
HE HE
HE
HE HE
E
HE
E

Messiah

he comes,
he comes,
of course it's a he
who comes,
postulated
by hordes of he's
from himhood immemorial,
he comes I tell you
to kiss the feet
of women,
to surrender his himliness
to women,
to unhim history
& will its words
to women,
& only incidentally
to vibrate the
polar antipodes
like the twin prongs
of a tuning fork

Mikhail Horowitz
ED 24

MY LOVE is

a saint,
a lustre of
earth,
comely as the milk of palestine

she is a palimpsest,
a fatal guest, the branches of
her body

a bibliography of jets & crevasses

my love is a grande route,
the autobahn without ghosts,

rumor of
a thousand lovers curves her lips

what a long melancholy gash of love
when she drops herself upon the couch

the child abandoned
to my care

a party of haute coiture, carried in by the valet
who says "don't touch, don't touch the silver bells

of those russet nipples!"

she is the sentry after fornication
the mountain of gems
the immobile air -

i am nothing, perhaps
a little farm boy
carrying eggs to market

Joel Lipman
ED 24

Winter Alba

Morning, too soon
sunlight bright
through the windows

The bed warm
wrapped each
in the other
we wake from
a common dream

Out into a
bitter cold
scrape the car windows
and begin
our separate days

Dennis Maloney
ED 24

Labor Day

Over this half moon black lake
live all the points of heaven
I knew by heart in the sixth grade

Tonight the constellations
mock my memory
A bat's shadow flits
low to the water

I stretch my eyes into
that space I
once saw as a ceiling
curved over my bed
in my first room
with a window

There are no loon cries
no rustling chipmunks
Somewhere deep in the woods
beyond the lake
a logging truck groans
at a hill

In the water must be
a fish too ready to catch
a bug ready to be eaten
a rock too long there
to be just a rock

High in the top
of that pine of Bluff Point
to the North of a star
whose name I have forgotten
is its highest needle

And in the jewel of moisture gathering
at its tip
Life becomes personal

Gary McLouth
ED 24

tonight,
the hoofbeats
of phantom horses
disturb my sleep,
scatter my dreams
of you:

stampeding madly
against my will
they drag my heart
behind them
through the dark,
raising great clouds
of confused, obscure
emotion:

invisible stallions
gallop in & out
of shadows.
i pick up my heart,
brush it off,
& wait for the dust
to settle:

thinking of you -
hearing the echoes
of the vanishing steeds,
feeling their strides
across my body,
wondering how
they can ever be tamed

Jack Shifflett
ED 24

February

everybody hates
this cold month

i love it
i love the groundhog
and persephone
her pomegranate seeds

i love valentine's day
the stupid cards

the coming up and
looking out
the reaching out
to touch another

i love my birthday
sitting in this month
      the woman said
aquarians always seem
older than they are

i said that's because
we're born early in
the year
            she said
oh you're right

i love the two days
every february
a wind blows gentler
and we know spring
will come to us
even though march
is waiting too

i love this month
your month
persephone
and yours you
ugly groundhog
and mine
        and lovers

Joel Oppenheimer
ED 24

mer maid

mer

mer

murmur to me of the sea

mer maid

mer

mer

maid of mer

made of sea

maid of mer/cy

maiden / me

sil/ver / mer/maid

maid of mer

maid of mar

made of mar/ble / statue/sque

made of mar

made of more

maid of mortal mem/or/y

maid of more

made of mir

maid of mir/rors

mere mirage?

wise-eyed / fish-tailed
/ mer/cur/y

mer maid

mer

mer

merge with me

maid of mer on mercy
seat

mer maid

mer

mer

mes / mer/ rising

rising / mur/mur

mer / maid / chant.

Linda Haggenjos
ED 25/26

Sacraments

We do not talk of God
as we light seven candles around the room
douse the artificial lights,
remove vestment after vestment
to find original skin.
We do not talk of God as we explore
ancient rites, annointing and sanctifying
each other on an altar of softness
slipping in and out of grace.
Yet God is here.

Nita Penfold
ED 25/26

Last Goddess on Earth

Starves in winter, learning to hibernate,
Gown covered with pennies, hair crinkled like an accordion,
Trees rattle their dry bones here,
Bones of her worshippers keep her awake.
Snow stretches across her doorway,
She writes on it stories from her life.

All of her sisters have died,
She can't cry anymore so she
Grows her arms long enough to wrap up the earth,
Washes her face in each ocean,
Arranges seaweed around her head like a crown,
Makes necklaces out of starfish,
Watches clouds drift towards each other like
Couples mating in daylight.

She melts her body down,
Becomes the jewelery young women wear,
Ruby eyes, silver teeth, filigree rings.
They all wear gowns like hers and
Practice being worshipped
While she watches alone, an evening star
Not letting them wish upon her.

She had no wishes or birthdays,
Put a mark on her heel for each day.
Marble was cold on her feet,
She covered them and lost track of the hours,
Following her sisters
Adjusting their crowns for them,
Daylight lasting for years.

Now her gown collects around her feet
Like a dry fountain.
She sits on her throne in a
Temple full of smooth stones,
If they were water they would freeze here
So far from sunlight.
She is tiny now, holding her own hands
Like beads in the necklaces with her emblem
Before they are buried for centuries.

Elaine Perry
ED 25/26

Prayer for Rain, or Something Else

We are not worthy -
(that's why we're asking) -
Lord, you give us the pleasure of life
the fruits of the Spirit
(the Lord giveth and the Lord taketh away)
why should we have it so hard?
                    //so soft?
                    //so hard?
                    //so soft?
so hard/in/soft?
into the depths I have cried unto Thee, oh God.
(and from out of these depths...
do I hear this?)

"Go directly to Hell.
"Thou shalt not pass GO.
"Thou shalt not collect $200, or any of the
                    benefits of His passion.
"You chose your own.

Adam delved//   Eve span.

and that mark - ?
the prince of the air (falling/forever falling/
ever closer) but not until the end of the
age will we see:
    Lord Christ w/the sword in his mouth
    The morning star do the ultimate crash-&-burn
and the instant that fruit was plucked,
    the leathery skin torn back,
    all the little red nubbles breaking forth,
    sucked out; the seeds, the evidence,
    clinging in the tangles of his beard;
That instant lasts forever. *It keeps happening.*
That choice never stopped being made
The fruit will never get past the gorge of
    Male & Female
until, in our flesh, we stand at the latter
day/and see Thee face to face.

    Amen, and Amen.

Robin Kay Willoughby
ED 25/26

Jack-In-The-Pulpit

(for Dr. Bill #1, Dr. Bill #2, and Bill)

That greeny, yellow-y,
purple-y,
not-
  quite
 flower

makes me think of fog-bound hills &
                    swamps
in spring; calls my self back to me
                in dark corners of
                the schoolyard

it's everything the opposite of pulpits - playing doctor,
                    never playing priest.

They say we go to dust, but seeing
this dark lily grow, I well suspect the earth to
which we turn is damp and rank,
and thuds too hard - fit
to wake the dead - on the boxes of
those come after.
I suspect Jack-in-the-pulpit's
poison:
        in the same bag w/mandrakes and
        tomatoes, milkweed, touch-me-not.

Jack, the pistil, stands serene & cool,
passive dangerous, meditating. Jack's
really female. [Form follows function, hon!
So, why so male, fond lover?]

I feel my very heart flutter open like that
waxy masquerade, and there,
                        in the depths of
rhythmic muscle, shivering, nude, is
little Jack.

Robin Kay Willoughby
ED 25/26

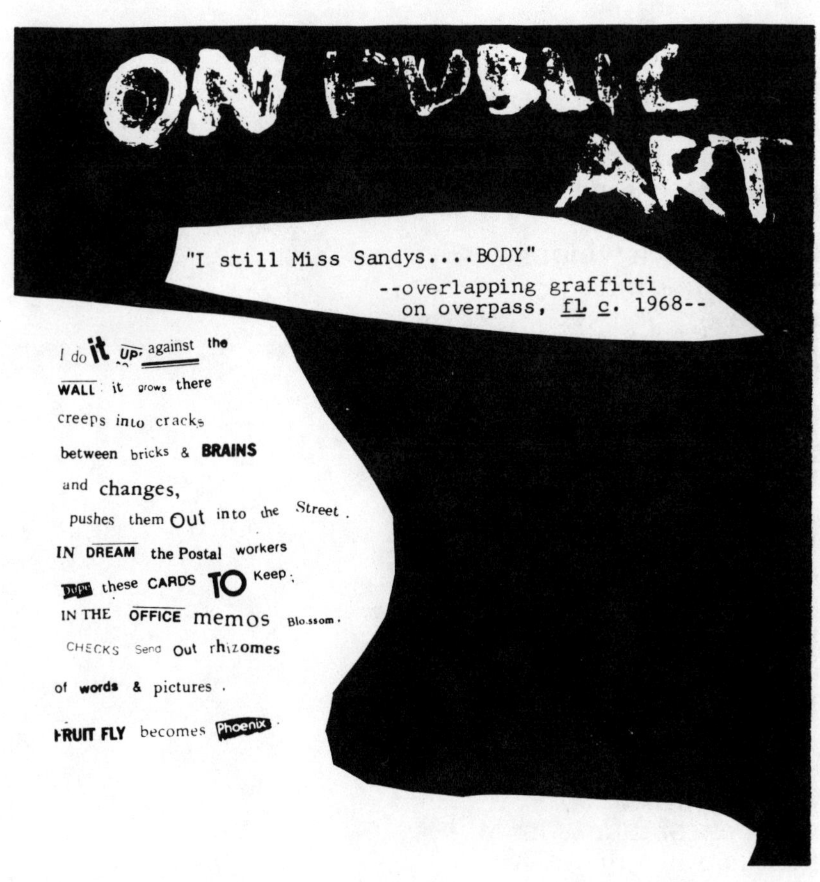

ON PUBLIC ART
"I still Miss Sandys....BODY"
--overlapping graffitti
on overpass, fl. c. 1968--
I do it UP against the
WALL it grows there
creeps into cracks
between bricks & BRAINS
and changes,
pushes them Out into the Street.
IN DREAM the Postal workers
these CARDS TO Keep;
IN THE OFFICE memos Blossom.
CHECKS Send Out rhizomes
of words & pictures.
FRUIT FLY becomes Phoenix.

Robin Willoughby
ED 17

A Hymn to Mourning

for Jean Donovan and the
three nuns murdered in
el salvador

1.

morning rain
sings black sobs
pre-dawn haze
casts a shadow
of the peace dove
the sole resident
in our church window
of red, blue, lime
and rose
now a window in the room
where we sleep
and dream

2.

morning grey
echoes rain
sob after sob
a chorus

this is not a dream

screams in the rain
do not mute the soft
whispers of four women
their fear neatly folded
in a missal/in frantic prayer
in a foreign field
to a God who abandoned them
praying for sleep
for sleep

3.

black morning
i hear bodies rustling
see Death
within the shadows
sacrificial red / martyred blue
i reach
to touch the rested faces
of four girl angels

Geri Grossman
ED 27

Breathing Calls I've Received

#1

With mouth open, with vocal chords
on during exhales, off during inhales,
with sounds approximating *uh:*

inhale, exhale; inhale, exhale;
inhale, exhale; inhale, exhale;
inhale, exhale; inhale, exhale.

Then say softly, as the *o* in "who"
and sustain through one very long breath:
"oooooooooooooooooooooooooooooo...."

#2

Say "Hello." Then, with lips fully
closed, rapidly and loudly click
the top of your tongue against your
soft palate. Alternately breathe
loudly through your nose, as

click, click, click.
inhale, exhale; inhale, exhale;
inhale, exhale.
click, click, click...

until the listener hangs up.

#3

Say seductively, softly, with lots
of breath:

"Hi sweety. Hey there?
How are you? Hello.
Hi there. You. Yes. You.
Hi, Sweety...."

Repeat infinitely. Allow the person
called to speak briefly at any point,
but answer only with this litany.

#4

Pucker your lips as for a kiss.
Inhale through the pucker
in short, continuous jabs of sound,
until you or the one called
gets too tired to continue.

#5

In a low crescendo of aspiration,
say *ah,* but do not turn on
your vocal chords when doing so, as

"ah, ah-, ah--, ah---,
Ah, Ah-, Ah--, Ah---,
AH, AH-, AH--, AH---"

Begin again as often as needed.
Alternate the size of your mouth
to vary the effects.

#6

Burp. Slurp. Hiccup.
Burp. Slurp. Hiccup.

#7

Make a series of clicks,
such as a cowboy makes
when he urges horses faster.
Punctuate rigidly thus:

2 sets of clicks. Silence.
3 sets of clicks. Silence.
2 sets of 7 clicks. Silence.
5 sets of single clicks. Silence.
Repeat indefinitely.

Li Min Hua
ED 27

8
8
88888
8
8 FENCES
8
8 8 8 8
8 8 8 8 8 8

After closing his shop,
Father would let my five girlfriends and me
hold hands in a chain
as the first one touched the sample strand
of barbed wire,
which electrified a little, then a little more,
then lots, right through our chain,
until one of us screamed.

Father would turn it off
while we all laughed and asked to try again.

That was in white Alabama
in 1943, during WW2,
when we bought our war bonds,
unquestioningly sat in the front of the bus,
and had not yet heard of other cattle prods
nor understood electrocution.

Li Min Hua
ED 27

Summer Mass

dream of the friends who save the earth
and the seas   there of
all the creatures
   that walk or swim

   answer the question
"what good is   a mosquito?"

do you believe   in   power?
do you believe   in the whale?
each named   by a tail

o flash that monicker and disappear
beneath the solid fog
betrayed by pelagic birds
who seek your food
disclosed by the need to breathe
we close our engines down and listen to the sea

obligation's
due the   too big
too small   too slow
ugly unmoving trees
in his dark retinal screen
no sight of the extremes of life
he wants the grass & berry eater
bunnies that kill   cute food
for us   not them

if there were right sky whales
they could strain the clouds of gnats
good change   upset a human wasp
see what you get!
rapid transit and extinction
instead of death's slow relocation

Kastle Brill
ED 27

He Said Her Bones

she wasn't much
bigger than the
doll she buried
her yelps in
I guess it hurt
it was hard
to open her her
mother at the
edge of the
hootch folding
the Yank bucks
Two weeks later
the place was
ash bodies
flaking like
dead moths
I thought at
least she
didn't die
a virgin

lyn lifshin
ED 27

The Rape

That's where it happened -
the windows are boarded up
like bandaged eyes.
He pulled me through an opening
into the basement,
turning me this way and that,
arranging me on the dirt floor
as if I were something to kill and eat,
peeling off my clothes
like skin.

With the light from the street lamp
shining on his knife
he pushed his penis into my mouth,
and then into the darkness
between my legs,
until I didn't know whether I was living
or had already died.

There's the myth about Persephone
carried off to the Underworld
while Demeter, her mother, isn't looking;
and the long night that follows,
the winter on earth.
When I got home
my mother washed the blood from my legs
and covered all the mirrors
as when a daughter dies.

Elaine Mott
ED 27

The Long-Distance Lover

Knows there is something beyond
The gunshot at the starting line
Loves running into the amethyst dawn
Can take the heat of the sun
And runs at the same time
Each day it seldom rains
Has learned to love running
In snow at midnight
Realizes that after any meet
There is always the coming home
And begins to suspect
This is a race without a finish line
Imagines instead some small torch
Or light, carried for awhile
Like a stopwatch pinned beneath the heart,
And then passed on
But knows the greatest wonder
May be some thing she may only guess
And wonder at, but never know.

Penelope Prentice
ED 27

LI'L TUFF GUY WEAR

Elise Alicia Bushmiller
ED 27

Ladies For Ferraro

Thinking it would be nice to see
a woman in the white house who
hadn't slept her way there, I
went to work for Mondale/Ferraro.

The first night they had me
making posters. That was fun.
I made the following posters:
"Ferraro - It's about time"
"We want Ferraro"
"Italians for Ferraro"
"You don't have to be
Italian to love Ferraro"

Then I remembered Mondale.
So I made a poster that said:
"Vote Ferraro/Mondale"
Then I made the following posters:
"Women for Ferraro"
"Feminists for Ferraro"

I wanted to make a poster that said:
"Dykes for Ferraro"
But I couldn't do it. Working at
the same table with me were
two women who looked like
Barbie dolls and I didn't
want to upset them.
One of the women couldn't think
of anything to write and
never did make a poster.
The other one thought hard
for a long time and
made a poster that said:
"Eastsiders for Mondale"

I'm from Brooklyn so I
made a poster that said:
"Brooklyn for Ferraro"
Then, because Ferraro is from Queens,
"Queens for Ferraro"
And that's the closest I ever got
to a poster that said:
"Dykes for Ferraro"

But I learned something very
important that night - how many
R's there are in Ferraro.

Rose Romano
ED 27

The Objects of Dreams

1

In dreams, objects receive themselves
We empty our flesh
in light,
in transformations, in voices.
Birds fly out of our sleeping eyes
and beat their wings ragged
against the unrelenting night.

Can you carry this dream?
Of the woman who travelled
with revolutionaries
into the El Salvador countryside?
She spoke on the news. All her words
flew like frightened sparrows
into the comfortable-Q-tipped-ears
of the bourgeoisie.

"We sat in a house surrounded by guns
and talked all night:
marriage, friendship, embroidery,
with the young student organizer.
She was just like me.
I was never so close to death before.
This young woman
who led us to safety,
away from the national guard,
died 10 days later, 2 days after her lover,
their bodies macheted,
their hands broken,
their genitals cut away, their eyes
torn out,"
their dreams

2 Gold

The trees turned totally,
gold and brilliant red flashing
off the outer leaves.
They cover the blue-tipped-spruce, gather
on the porch roof with the winged seeds,
drift to clog the drain.
A chipmunk bellies
the wet slate walk.
The marigold's charred blossoms sag

on wrenched stems.

Curious, how the flame
that in the gold leaf
pleases, in my mother
scares us.
Crouched,
holding her face, her stray
frizzed irradiated hair
she whimpered like a child.
"Why did you get out of bed?"
we cried, my father and I,
my father whirling in the room,
"O Betty, Betty, we don't *need* this!"
Then, "Don't panic!" talking to himself.

I saw the wound welling ruby,
short gouge on her brow,
one stitch,
no danger.

Can there be
danger, when so slowly
she goes, part of her offering
disease humble and ugly,
part of her wishing
to love to
love her life?

We are small sad creatures
and cannot understand our lives.

3 Gold Again

Gold in coffers,
gold in peacock's eyes
gold beaten into chains and bands,
slaves beaten into holes in the ground
for gold.
Gold in the center of daisies,
gold in the open hands of maple trees,
gold flowing in veins,
gold in the fingertips
nicotine translucent
as she fumbled her cigarette,
gold wedding band
gold necklaces she bought
when she knew she was sick

and did not believe,
gold urine I flush
as she stands and fumbles her pants
not quite so dizzy
gold threads in the fancy wallpaper
I trace with my hand
as I guide her through the light
gold floods on the living room rug
we wade through
surprised.

4

In dreams, objects receive themselves.

The corpses sit up and spit blood-drained words.
White, silent like the neat skeletons of fish,
they lie bone by bone beneath
the layering silt of riverbottoms.
Other disappeared persons float anonymous,
serene in their eyelessness.
These objects do not stare, cannot speak.
In my dreams they receive themselves.
The empty flesh repopulates.

I am going to tell you a story
about a woman who dies a long time
before leaving her body.
It lies curled on her bed, bald,
a few frizzled hairs grown back.
the eyes blink, the hands crawl up her chin,
they pat her lips.
The woman sits and smiles at strangers.
But they are not strangers.
They are her sons, her husband, her friends,
and she has neglected farewell.
She has escaped.
Her eyes blink. Her lips smile.
Her restless fingers
pat and pat her cheeks.

5

In dreams, objects receive themselves.
This is a dream of a body without a soul.
The woman, my mother,
who believed in justice,
in helping children find happiness,

in helping parents find themselves,
my mother whose youngest son steals from her
and wants her to love him anyway
goes out of her body.
she empties her flesh.
Is there a right or wrong in this?

Is it like taking a young woman outraged by murder
and filling her vagina with nails or hot water
or electricity?
Is it like taking a child and beating her stomach
until it bursts,
in front of her mother who has nothing
to tell,
no stories, not even lies?
Is it like being a man who throws birds
head-first at walls
to hear the delicate click of the neck bones
snapping?

These are the objects of our dreams:
my mother, her escape,
this man, his bird, this child
her burst stomach, her mother,
the young girl, her vagina,
the hands of the men
who pick her up and slam her down,
the calloused skin of their thumbs,
the odd ache in his back of the one
who wakes at dawn remembering
where a boy once hit him
with a stone.

These beings empty themselves
into our sleep.
They are dark feathers beating against
the windows of our nights,
begging to be let in.
Are there words
to mend this?
Are there words
to change
this?

6

In dreams, objects receive themselves,
and we empty our flesh

in light,
in transformation,
in voices.

Light transforms itself
Voices touch one another.

Can this light outshine the dark?
Can any song carry this dream?
Could I suffer those wounds
and still dream?
Do these dreams spell themselves
across *your* pillow too?
What voices populate *your* nights?
Can they kindle a fire
a dance for the tongue?
Can you, or I,
possibly be silent?

Susan Fantl Spivack
ED 27

DOUBLE SOLSTICE STAR

Judith McCombe
ED 27

Eve & Adam 1980

Young & lovely they live
in New York City: she writes
& he paints late into the night
& together they watch
through a plant-studded window
the lights of the Empire State Building
flash off at midnight: red-blue-white.

I've heard them say they eat
quantities of pasta
with nuts & oil & garlic & basil
he grinds with a wooden pestle,
she mixes with good pale cheese;
but they are thin with the luxury
of living on each other's dreams.

They may marry
but will not have children.
They may sell their plants
but will keep cuttings.
They may move from New York City
but will never leave this place:

her desk, his easel,
the memory of a tower of light
shining until midnight.

Katharyn Machan Aal
ED 28

Choices

I want to wake up
alone grief
as old as April snow
as cold
burning now
as crocus spears
into light no

pain
is greater than
winter dreams seared
by spring the thin
vanilla'd air no

pain
is greater than
forging this poem
firing
a future or
staying with you
and living in snow
in snow
in snow
in snow.

Nancy Barnes
ED 28

He Is Like Goldfish

You know, those cheesy
little crackers that

you don't know you
want until you've tried

one, then two, take
a small scoop, then

fold up the bag; but
maybe a few more would

be nice so you unfold it
and you take another scoop

and you fold up the bag
and you sit to watch t.v.

and you can't wait for a commercial
and before it comes

you open the bag again,
and fold it closed,

and you walk away,
and turn back,

and you unfold it again
and you've got the bag in one hand

and you pour the crackers
into the other,

and you put the handful
into your mouth

and you keep filling your hand
and shoving them into your mouth

until there are about
five left and then you

eat one by one,
cracking them in half

in your mouth, sucking
the insides you've never seen;

Then there's only
one left,
so you place it
on your tongue

and chew it up
and know you need a drink

of water or
juice or something,

but you don't want
to lose that taste.

Jeanine Van Voorhees
ED 28

The Prolific Poet

for lyn

you can't even shut the
self-addressed stamped
envelope/it sticks
to the poems and you
gotta roll it down/tape it
and try to keep the
wad of paper under control
at the same time

getting them *out* is
bad enough/glue sticking to
the edges of the sheets//
tore the tops off six
poems the last time and it
still took an hour to
read them all/don't know
how you can get so
many pieces of paper
into one #10 envelope

whenever I see yr name
in the corner I groan/gol
dang it/woman//will you
please control yrself

Bonnie Johnson
ED 28

An Illustrated History

of the morning night

When she had not yet seen the dogs

and came home with the wrong man

to a laundry covered bed

that was another time

when it was noones dream

©1979 B KASTLE BRILL

separately they rise

and meet awake

KASTLE

Kastle Brill
ED 10/11

from Litany of the Clothes

WOMAN #1

Pearl has taken a vow of pants. She will not wear skirts until the male members of the Psychology Department at the State University of New York at Buffalo wear skirts and the state of their legs is remarked upon. She figures it'll be a lifetime vow. This is what Pearl has given up: twirling in featherlight materials and wind on her thighs and a certain freedom and a certain grace and garter belts with tiny blue flowers on them and nylon stockings and colorless nail polish dabbed on runs and red taffeta crinolines and twirling and a certain safety and a certain vulnerability and lace garters and groomed legs and a certain link with women and pink razors and nicks and cuts and blood and blood stoppers that sting like hell and stubble and pink electric shavers and a certain power and the skin he loves to touch and waxes and creams and depilatories and electrolysis and a certain privilege and little girls holding her train and skirts looped to the arm like empresses and sweeping into rooms and a certain mystery and rustling and organdy and a man screaming at her for using his razor and mini and midi and maxi and micro and a stranger sliding his hand down and up and pretending it's not happening and slips versus no slips half slips mini slips pettipants teddies and a certain link with herself and twirling and static cling and little boys trying to look up her skirts and an appropriate curtsying costume and curtsying and vulgar remarks and crossed legs in public and don't bend over panties showing and slips showing and ratings on a scale from 1 to 10 and sometimes winning and always losing and goosebumps and chilblains and leg lotions and fear of thick ankles and fear of fat calves and fear of wobbly thighs and fear of bowlegs and fear of knobby knees and fear of scars and fear of warts and fear of birthmarks and blemishes and being imperfect and leg make-up and suntan front and back matching and limbs so shiny and sleek people can hardly keep their hands off them and most of all the twirling.

WOMAN #4

Daisy wears a white lace dress and rides around the field at halftime. The weather is perfect, the breeze plays on Daisy's bare shoulders and arms but never disturbss her hair, the dress is perfect, the city dress her sister drove 80 miles for, never has anyone in the town seen such a dress, Daisy lives that brief shifting moment in time when the girl and the woman use the same body simultaneously. Three times they circle the field, round and round and round: the people will not let them go. Dutch Schultz, the captain of the football team, waits with the flowers. Home team is behind 12 points. Dutch Schultz's face, his blue and white uniform, are streaked with mud, his eyes are serious. Daisy leans down from the haunch of the silver convertible to receive the roses. Daisy is so close to Dutch Schultz she smells his sweat rising sweet sweeter than the burning leaves and the blood red roses. The applause grows so loud only Daisy hears Dutch say, "I'll win it for you." *(Pause)* He wins it for her.

WOMAN #7

Ohhh, how sweet.

WOMAN #6
Tell us some more.

WOMAN #2
(from pedestal without change of expression) I told you the best part.

WOMAN #4
Pictures shot from the bleachers reveal two inches of cleavage. Daisy buys up all the photos and tears them into microscopic pieces. The rest of Senior year, Daisy wears blouses buttoned all the way up. Dutch Schultz sells prints off the negative. "How's tricks?" Dutch Schultz says to Daisy every time he passes her in the hall.

Gabrielle, Maria, & Jennifer Burton
ED 29

Query

Was this my first stop in the New World?
        A fresh, wet head
        (skull bones like continental plates)
        laid on softness,
                like this,
        reassured by familiar cadence?

Was this where I fell asleep,
        again and again,
                like this,
        replenished?

Is it my oldest memory
        that you revive,
        which makes this place
        comforting
                beyond words?

Elizabeth B. Conant
ED 30

Parable 25

The Abbess has fallen
not from the grace of God
for only her Prioress
knows the color of her hair
but from grace of Goddess
concerned with Sister Almond
named for the shape of eyes
and tears constantly salting
the full-bodied tiles of chapel.

The Abbess has fallen
from her right to indignity,
to cross red legs under
the robes of the judgment seat,
to visit after compline
rooms of trusted friends,
squeeze hands groping for perfection,
kiss cheeks inflamed
with love for the Christ
and feel superior

while Sister Almond
tries to flagellate away
the mellow lushness of her skin,
propping toothpicks in eyes
hoping for death at twenty.

Thomas Kretz
ED 30

This Is A Poem

This is a poem

This is a poem for

This is a poem for Mrs. Crowley
whose face I cannot remember

This is a poem for Mrs. Crowley
whose blue/veined/scratched fingers
passed out the paper, one sheet to a child

This is a poem for Mrs. Crowley, *NO MISTAKES NOW*
who watched over my skinny shoulder
as I fumbled to pencil the apple and banana
propped on Sister Alicia's desk

This is a poem for Mrs. Crowley who clicked her tongue
against the roof of her mouth and shook her head
until the fluorescent lights seemed to flicker & fade

This is a poem for Mrs. Crowley who clicked her tongue
and pronounced *YOU CAN'T DRAW* as if that was all
there was to it until the end of time//
and something closed up small inside me

This is a poem for Mrs. Crowley

This is a poem for

NO

This is a poem

This is a poem for longing

This is a poem for all the longing
locked inside these fingers

This is a poem for the morning glories
I would not draw

This is a poem for the pale pink of dawn reflected
in their fluted mouths, the little trumpets that folded
up into fans on pale stems in the broad light

This is a poem for their thick green stalks topped
with the fierce orange I burned brightly within me

This is a poem

YES

This is a poem

This is a poem for Amy with the paint-soaked rags

This is a poem for Amy at college where
Beginning Art meant that you already were capable

This is a poem for Amy who painted at night
because she couldn't work with all those fish/eyes
staring in the open bowl of studio

This is a poem for Amy who taught me to play
with light & shadow, pen & ink
and who tried to make Mrs. Crowley's voice go away

This is a poem for Amy

This is a poem

YES

This is a poem

This is a poem for my daughters
who had crayons and paper before they could walk

This is a poem for my daughters who colored
& cut & ripped & played

This is a poem for my daughters who had oil pastels,
modeling clay, wood, yarn, fabric scraps, egg cartons,
poster paint, chalk, felt-tip markers, and seventeen
different weights and textures of paper culled
from garbage cans and garage sales

This is a poem for my daughter, Sara, who drew
the inside of a chestnut at the age of four

This is a poem for my daughter, Kate, who
drew a book of faces before she was three

This is a poem for my daughters whose teachers
say *YES, your drawings are good*
YES, your lines are clean, your composition fine

This is a poem for my daughters

YES

This is a poem for them

Nita Penfold
ED 30

In Cahoots With The Frizz

I bend my head over the sink and brush
then lift my eyes to the mirror to find
you standing straight up
all twelve or so inches of you.
I say "you look like I just put my finger
in a light socket," and grin.
Sometimes I put my glasses back on
and we laugh, co-conspirators in a war
on fashion.

After all the compliments we got when you
were curly and short, you decided it was time
to go long again. You're bolder than I.
When somber women say "long hair is a sign
of passing for straight," you roll my eyes,
we chortle to ourselves. Passing for straight?
You'll never pass for straight.
You're incorrigible. You're something
to live up to.

Susanna J. Sturgis
ED 30

Portrait of Joseph Clovis Despault

Lean and gaunt, my grandfather, and his children too. Narrow, angular faces, long jaws and high brows, scant and fragile hair that thins early. Bony hands I recall, unfolding around the dime for the movies, fingers long and aristocratic: the hands of a man who works with his head, not his back. He goes walking every day from his narrow city house, a slender shadow in a charcoal suit, strands of pale hair neatly covered by his black hat. A tidy man, my grandfather, who presses his trousers himself, aligning the crease precisely with the fine gray stripe in the worsted wool. Daily he walks to the bank where he spends his hours filling narrow-ruled ledgers with column after column of delicate flourished numerals. Sometimes there is a look of distance in his eyes, their brilliant blueness gone opaque. My parents tell me it's because his mind is somewhere else.

* * * * * *

A city child, I am vaguely aware of birds, the fitful flight of duncolored sparrows, the flashes of oily iridescence on pewter pigeons. My world is enlarged one autumn afternoon as my grandpapa and I leave leaden skies outside to wander among the exhibits in a museum of natural history. I am entranced before panoramas that mimic nature: a mountain lion menaces on the flaking layers of a shale projection; a fox mother stands beside the dark plaster hole that shelters her kits; beavers posture stiffly, working on a birchwood dam in a mirrored pond. Most enchanting, the crayola plumage of birds, whose strange names he reads for me. We fill ourselves with the exuberance of chartreuse, mauve and lemon; memorize the elegant cobalt drape of a tail patterned with green-rimmed eyes; a cluster of wispy orange feathers explodes into an extravagant arched cascade.

We stand a long time there, gazing in companionable silence. This grandfather is not at ease making small talk with a small girl, but I sense his kindness. My mind still explores the afternoon's treasures as we hurry home in the drizzling dusk. My hand fits comfortably in his.

* * * * * *

There are so many trees here, it looks like a park to me. I wait in the car while my parents visit my grandfather, who now lives in the large white building at the far end of a curving drive. Grandpapa is here, I am told, because he is ill and needs the care of nurses, and I am too young to visit. My parents have brought him a shopping bag full of metal lids from five-gallon lard tins, and they return with just one given in exchange. Using the rim as a frame, my grandfather has painted a picture on it, filling the circle with whorls of petals layered thickly one upon another, a fantasy of passionate colors. He paints to pass the time. This picture does not look like my quiet grey grandpapa.

* * * * * *

Memories of this man are tender beyond the fragments of knowledge I have of him. They are a child's response to shyness, quiet voice and gentle touch. I am a woman grown before I understand that his vibrant bouquets are reflections of grandpapa's rainbow-hued spirit, freed from its physical boundaries. More than his blood and bones are mine. His yearnings are alive in my own soul.

Camille Cox
ED 31/32

SOMETHING TO CRY ABOUT

I'll give you something
to cry about he'd shout
grabbing my wrist and twisting
my arm up high
behind my back

Tears and pleading didn't work
so I turned to taunts instead:
Go ahead!
Break it if it makes you
feel good

which of course
made him madder
and he'd jerk it higher
My mother cried
and tried to pull him off

but he shoved her out of reach
Gotta teach her a lesson
Too smart for her own good
Give her something
to cry about

I was a picked-clean wishbone
waiting for the sound
of my own bones dryly snapping
Like the clapping after a concert
it would finally be over

Face-down in the pillow afterward
I wondered who would be left
with the biggest piece who
would be the lucky one
which one of us would win.

Kathryn Daniels
ED 31/32

JEDEDIAH: A SLANT RHYME

Think of him as a silk scarf,
white and wrapped about a woman's neck,
tossed by a wind that first licks,
then whips and steals,
tears the scarf off and sets it free.
The woman, chilled now, screeches.
She chases the scarf; it flies,
laughing, a bird, a cloud, a ribbon,
loosed in the cobalt blue sky, then drops upon
a car's antenna and wraps itself tight.
The woman, breathless, stops short
just before the car, furious,
but warmed by the race, turns curious.
"What is this scarf?" she snorts
then rips it down, beautiful silk,
now soiled, wrinkled, twisted, yet,
it's her scarf, her baby, her pet.
She tucks it in, thrilled
not to have lost the thing
she can not match.
Think of him as that silk scarf.

Nancy Bengis Friedman
ED 31/32

THE GAME

"Catch up."

The words hang in the air ahead,
Signals in the foggy four o'clock
Summoned whole in recollected time.
That inch or two of detailed memory
Is taking me again, over the same
Half-frozen ground.

"Catch up."

I stop, confronted where I stand.
The voice I quicken to, obedient as a hound,
Still works.

And Father, memorized, appears.
Huge, deft-footed he's ahead,
Moving fox quiet, red hair flickering,
Threading in and out of trees,
Bark shag becomes his camouflage.
He half-turns, beckoning.

"Catch up. Come on."

Swift, he is away again,
Shoulders streaming in gelid air,
Disappearing even as I watch him go.

It is our family game.
He learned it tracking, Indian-style,
In his father's wake,
Long ago and bitter cold in Mississippi sloughs,
And played dead serious
On spent late autumn afternoons, like this.

I've lost him.
Shadow, he's parted the bark-rough curtain
And stepped inside.

"Catch up."

It hushes in the pines.
I squint, and chafe my stiffened hands,
Wipe my crusted, swollen eyes,
Wait where last I heard the voice,
Scarce breathing, still feverish to obey.

Ahead, above, I think I see him.
Braced in the feathery blur of hemlock crotch
He lolls, at ease.

Lifting a brown, thick-calloused palm, peremptory,

"Climb up."

Summoned, I am ordered there.
It is the test.

Boots sliding, scrambling to find purchase,
I climb bare-handed.
Blood-urged to win, I fail.
I was expected to.

I learned to play the game at twelve.
Armed with a girl-child's easy grace
I found the hemlock first and made the climb.
And straddling there in Father's place
I called, "Come up," to him below.

Peering, he fixed me with an adversary's stare,
Taking my measure behind hooded eyes.
Then, hunching his heavy shoulders,
He turned and left me there.

Perrie J. Hill
ED 31/32

1949 PONTIAC

black and sleek
my father rounds
sparkle of chrome
on gleaming fastback
mother tucked inside
the vault
like slam of
the door still
dancing in his ears
solid as a limo
this secret joe dimaggio
about to cruise away
with marilyn.

Eileen Moeller
ED 31/32

LESSONS

Father taught me the useful arts:

how to curse in Gaelic,
how to drink Tullamore Dew
without choking,
how to cash checks
at Penguin's Five & Dime,
how to survive
on forty dollars a week,
how to brew tea strong enough
for a mouse to run across it.

After years of silence,
he believes I have forgotten him.
He does not know that I remember
each time I scour my darkened cup.

Patricia Nesbitt
ED 31/32

INCEST

Incest
is a taboo,
which says nothing
about the damage done,
which says nothing
about recollecting
an organdy-curtained,
wallpaper-bowered
bedroom,
shades drawn against the
early evening light and heat,
which stream through nonetheless,
glaring around the edges
like mica chips in desert sand
at noon.

To speak
of a taboo
does not speak
to the damage done
by and experience
which cannot be
remembered whole
but rather,
comes in bursts
of recollection
like sand drawn up
by desert wind
to smack dead
against
a freshly painted
white clapboard house
in the middle of
the oasis on
the Old Mormon Trail.

To speak of the damage done
by violating a taboo
will never do justice
to an experience
whose recollection
centers on
a father
and his nine-year old
daughter,
who grew up
surrounded by
oleanders in crimson
and white bloom,
by blue chase trees and
clusters of brilliant red
pyracantha berries,
near proud stand of
iris, not far from
formal rose gardens
sprouting out of
dirt
trucked in from southern California
over the Baker grade
and dumped on top of
a fragile ecosystem
never meant to sustain
a dimly recollected experience
based on a broken taboo.

Sarah Slavin
ED 31/32

TO HER HUSBAND, *from THE RED DUST SERIES*

To Her Husband

I wipe red dust from the white window sill.
He told me, nothin' will grow here.
How could I be prepared -
the dust blows through the screen.
You can't be concerned with keepin' a house clean,
the neighbors tell me.
I wipe the counter.
I'm from Connecticut.
        green hills roll under my back
        my breasts ache

Wyoming. Indian and outlaw names - Sundance,
Cheyenne. Dirt names-Muddy Gap, Rock Springs.
Nothing sounded like Hartford as we drove
and drove the land
empty,
I became empty,
a wild antelope.
He didn't see it.
I didn't pity it. So empty.
We carried it to the side of the road.
It was still warm. We left it there-warm.
I let myself grow cold against the wind.

I wipe red dust from the white window sill,
squeeze the rag into the sink.
A swirl of red against white.
I rinse the rag,
and wipe, and wipe the counter.

Marie Cartier
ED 33/34

ENTERING THE SURROUNDINGS

Entering the surroundings
one does not speak.
One enters into the chickadee
eating alder seeds
upside down,
and into the dry crunch of snow underfoot.
Enters into the pale moon above the mountains.
Enters into the cold,
the dogs' howls echoing from the ravine
where water dreams and thrashes its legs
under the ice.
Loses one's self entering.
Enters one's self.

Ann Fox Chandonnet
ED 33/34

SHAMAN

Shadowed against tin walls
at midnight dusk,
she whips cloudberries and seal oil
into ice cream.

Cloudberries fell from sky-country,
sockeye red they landed on tundra,
bits of sky
cooled and sweetened.

"Take. Eat." offers Caribou Woman,
after a long drag
on her Virginia Slim.

lola danet
ED 33/34

NO MERCY

Finally Eleanor decided to kill her houseplants.
She just couldn't take their dusty green hands held up to her, pleading for love.
She had read somewhere that they liked music,
and that they screamed when they were cut,
and wished to be moved about gently.
They were terribly sensitive.
So she thought she would try
to make the end merciful, somehow.
In the late fall, she set them
out in the yard, in dignified rows,
then ran back to the house, shut the door tight.
"Tonight they'll freeze," she thought.
"They'll fall into a nice green sleep.
There will be no screaming or carrying on.
Just a nice sleep."
Then came Indian Summer - warm days
and nights for nearly two weeks.
Eleanor was miserable; the suspense was awful.
She had wanted it to be over fast,
like the electric chair, like most hangings.
Defeated, she brought them back inside,
set them in their regular places,
gave them a little drink,
and a dirty look.

from Eleanor Moosehart

Sally A. Fiedler
ED 33/34

POOR FARM

I learned conservation from my parents
Counting every scrap on my dinner plate.
"You're sending us to the poor farm," they said,
Watching me eat, tallying the waste while
I wrestled down cabbage, red rice, turnips,
The wretched menu of thrift. I could see
Our family was the only one saving.
My friends refused broccoli and bolted
Desserts; our careless neighbors were packing
For the poor farm but they always returned
Tan and fat. I didn't know one person
Who ever went; I lost my faith early,
But last night I watched a poor-farm report
Because the last one in Minnesota
Was being razed. There were still photographs
Of ruined miners, sweat shop survivors,
Men with black lung lost among vegetables
And livestock. They worked this farm of Babel;
They spoke everything but English and died
Holding onto an untranslated pride.
All along somebody had been reaching
The poor farm, twelve-hour days in makework fields.
None of them believed in welfare, so much
Like my parents reheating residue
Of bargains. The last, living resident
Spoke from a nursing home, ninety-seven,
Surprised by leisure. He said Roosevelt
Murdered the spirit of men and listed
What he'd harvested: carrots, tomatoes,
Rutabagas, squash. "Any old God-damned
Thing you can think of," and widened his mouth
Into long, toothless laughter for himself,
My parents, disbelief of the wasteful.

Gary Fincke
ED 33/34

Judith Treible
ED 2

MUIR WOODS, 1984

Sitting at my kitchen table,
the supper dishes almost cleared,
I close my eyes to briefly rest them.
Outside squalls a summer thunder storm,
its raindrops carried to me on cool breezes
dampening my skin through broken screens
and open windows.
Then, just that quickly, I am back
in Muir Woods among tall Redwood trees,
transfixed again, as I was then,
and just as mute to name the magic.
I only say there is an awesome hush
that emanates from primal soil and ancient wood
in Muir forest.

I wonder at this sudden ease of travel
for I have tried before retracing steps,
reviewing vistas.
As any traveler has, I have my store
of photographs and postcard scenes, images
too bright, too dark, too brown, too red, too light.
None ever bear the fragrant scents
which weighted down the forest air,
nor emanate the cool and damp,
nor any trace of feeling there.

I sit motionless, afraid to move
lest movement break the spell and send me
tumbling home. Even so, my eyelids open.
Outside, the storm's subsided;
the clouds disperse, and now the breeze blows hot,
disturbs the space in which I sit
and brushes crumbs from off the table.
I see supper dishes still to clear.
There is no Muir Woods,
there are no redwoods here.

Barbara Ann Porte-Thomas
ED 33/34

THE DAUGHTERS OF COPPER WOMAN

No one noticed when they slipped away,
running over moss-covered earth at night,
deeper and deeper into the forest
until they faced themselves.

For years they hid
in caves, under trees,
sucking sap and chewing bark.
At night they listened
to their sisters scream
from the towns, from villages, waiting
till it was safe to return.

Later they moved back silently, gliding
through the streets, eyes
like agates.

When they speak
their words burn: one day
you will wake up wondering
who you are and where you are going.

The daughters of copper woman
will be waiting to show you.

Lily-Iona Soucie
ED 33/34

ATALAYA

Atalaya, Peru, August 1986

Arch of the foot
over the stones from the river
arch of the foot
over the round stones from the river
on the road of dust and stones
it's one o'clock
jungle time, and there's no way out
no flights, no boats, the sun
a grill on the tin roofs

from the warm bench
the clouds,
realities inside other realities,
surfaces turning over while we sleep
and time stops
enormously slow time cranks to a halt
and the feet seek out the stones
the stones from the river

enchantment sits in the trees
in the growing bush and the cries of the cock
her fingers reach out from the branches
of the mamei in the plaza
of the mango and the cashew
the little clothes, hanging from hooks
in the market, rock in the wind

time stopped, the wind sweeps the plaza
and the slow rolling laugh of the mother
under the river moves the stones
there is no way out
no place other than here
no time other than now
the slow beating of the heart

a curious tenderness in the perimeters
of the web she weaves
all her children are happy
nailed to the wall

the woman, like trees walking, are all satisfied
with the proud eyes of savage birds
they watch the river

the wind over the plaza brings the news
we've already heard more than once
no planes come in, no planes go out
no canoes, no boats
time stops
there is no way out of the jungle today.

Janine Pommy Vega
ED 33/34

REHEARSING FOR WAR

she packs every day,

wondering what refugees did
for clean underwear

she practices in the trek to work
with spare socks
shoes to walk in

and an empty notebook
for history and art

paper will be value then

like diamond rings and fertility
cannot decide if she could pass
when her hair comes in grey

will they, like bad novels
come to life,
call her "old woman"

without protector she returns
to the old game
avoiding the notice of men

she plans to return to old books
herbal cures and magic
to learn craft and healing

for in spite of what the army says
no one will need lawyers
after the war

Kastle Brill
ED 35

THE OFFSPRING

Behind the well house,
someone's cousin
revealed exactly
how our parents
conceived us,
and when I swore
it wasn't true,
he tossed a horseshoe
around an iron stake
and walked away
from its cold ringing.

All afternoon
I sat upon a fence,
watching a mare play
sweetly with her foal,
and when the stallion
nudged me for the sugar
in my pocket,
I rose and
ran away, crying
no, no, no.

Marie Connors
ED 35

THE SECRET

"Fluid Italian suede
in garnet,"
the copy croons.
I memorize the Bergdorf Goodman
catalogue,
the blonde with garnet lips
carrying my pocketbook
against her slim hip.
270 dollars.
One rent check,
one chunk of my daughter's
college.
After weeks of foreplay
I sell out my family,
dial the toll-free number.
It's miraculously
easy, just "ten working-days"
and here it is, wrapped
in tissue paper, nestled
in a silk carrying case.
For days I hide it
behind the recliner,
playing peek-aboo,
trying it out when my husband's
not home.
Nothing else in my life's
this beautiful.
To keep it
I would have to buy
silk suits, tweed coats,
a silver Porsche,
house on Park Avenue.
My shoulders are unworthy
of the thick strap
in wine-red suede,
I would have to have inches
surgically added to my height.
"American women carry
their souls
in their pocketbooks,"
Edgar Allen Poe wrote.

Not just my soul,
my money,
my identity,
my credit cards.
This pocketbook soft
and red like a vulva,
like a womb,
room where I could
carry myself in comfort,
be my own mother,
be drunk with color,
270 dollars.
I could sell my
wedding ring,
break into neighbor's
houses, after two years
in the women's
correctional facility
there it would be
waiting for me
fluid Italian suede
in garnet,
big enough to carry
the collected works of Poe,
o my fair sister, o my soul.

Marilyn Kallet
ED 35

JUNKOBODY THE BROOMMAN

Junkobody the Broomman
sweeps in circles.
When children call his name,
it's not the real one.
He does not remember the real one.
"Ragpan! Hey, Dustball!
Junkobody's got a fat old woman!
Stuffs her full of marbles and old mothballs!"
Junkobody laughs,
shows the places used to be teeth.

"Don't call Old Moldy, John,"
whispers fourth grade wiseass.
"Last time anyone called him John,
he beaned him with his dustpan,
put him in his closet." Junkobody's
closet: noone's seen it.
Full of mummies, anybody ever
called him a real name.
Also, hairribbons, rulers,
rags, love notes.
"Meet me after, by Junkobody's bicycle."
Moldy John knows what they're up to,
waits by his bicycle, knocks them down,
calls names: "Slushy Susie, Bramble Bobby.
"Don't cry, want to see my broomstick?
Want to see me fly?" Their tears
make shallow dark pocks in the dust.
"Don't tell," he whispers.
Takes out his long
handled broom.
Rides away whistling: "Don't tell."

Keeps the button
he popped off Bobby's shirt,
the barrette slid out of Susie's hair.
Takes them to his fat old woman.
She hugs him. "O, John!" in the hallway.
"What you got for me today?"
She's almost full up,
but she wants more; he gives her.

"O, John."
She takes him by the broomstick
rides him far.
"O John."

No little voices.
No funny names.
Junkobody forgets he is their broomman.
They think
he's got gold in his closet.

Susan Fantl Spivack
ED 35

WHAT NOBODY KNOWS

She is hanging upside-down
in the orchard, all alone in the fog.
Her pigtails touch tips
with the grass blades.
They all drip together
on this morning thick with secrets
and the shout of a pair of red shorts
swinging from an apple tree.

She loves looking at the world
downside-up.
The scabby bark of her branch
scratches the backs of her knees
but she hangs on a little longer,
running her short fingers
through the hillside's damp fur.
Deep in the distance
a crow hollers twice.

They will call her in before long.
She will be told to take a bath
and put on a dress.
Her mother will towel her hair
too roughly
and set her down by the stove.
She will be questioned
and remarked upon, and her answers
will be as wrong as her looks.

But the hour is still early
and now she is an apple
bright among the drooping leaves,
the shy, retreating tree trunks,
one of the secrets of the mist
and not for anyone to touch.

Ann Goldsmith
ED 35

A SHAPE SOFT ENOUGH TO WEAR

She is a woman
who lived three hundred years ago.
There was so much crying
in her hair, and yet,
two women together
can sometimes laugh so hard,
moments are strung together
and no one falls behind.

In her diary she mourns
friends left behind in England.
A house destroyed by fire
robbed her of the only books she had.
The newest child was teething
and threw up in the preacher's hand.
"July the 11th. - Hollyhocks bloomed,
a purple so dark it seemed a shadow
of a flower." So she seems to me

purple, breaking a bedroom mirror,
watching a garden of sharp flowers
grow at her feet. She was ready
to tuck them around her wrist,
but something moving in her eye
made her look another way.

Two women can talk the night
into a shape soft enough to wear
one more time. It's almost as if
the same onion planted over & over,
never decays, grows like a prayer.

We seem so close, she and I.
My hands could overlay hers
as the bread is kneaded. Three loaves
set in the sun to rise. Each day
begins with these small movements.
Even in a cracked mirror, they shine.

Lynn Martin
ED 36

CONFESSION

I confess
I flew over three time zones
to get here on time
shedding hours as if I'd
been living beyond my years

they lied
told me this old man
struck cancer dumb
was my father

I stayed
because my mother thought
he was her husband

outside
sheets of newspaper
floated in the duststorm
like prehistoric birds

light became a dense purple
eating the mesa
leaving only a great
purple bruise

how fragile each breath
seems when it may be the last

I confess that while I listened
to the falter and catch of each one
I told myself to watch carefully
miss nothing

I confess
I knew what I was doing
I would remember until
it was safe, until later
when I could think
rather than feel

this man waited until
the day I got here
with my impeccable timing
he raises his cool, dry hand
closes it over my own
like a baby might

for months those birds
of silence have circled
everytime I sat to write

I wait for
plangorous voices
to break from
those vacant throats

the grief of orphans
is for themselves
I confess that while
this stranger died
I drew his last breaths
into a poem
with every detail
I could salvage from
this barren desert
to distract me

I did what I had to
I confess

Helen Ruggieri
ED 36

MEDICINE MAN

Denims corrugated
as his face, the engineer
scrapes his boots
in the dust of failure.
The cap he wears to hide his eyes
advertises nothing.

Shaman once, he waits
out the promise of rain.
The little girl died anyway
even though her cancer
has gobbled up part of his singing.

Pamela Clements
ED 37

AUNT HELEN'S BOOKS

My father brought romance with meals on wheels.
He carried my dead aunt's books to invalids.
And those women in housecoats picked at meatloaf,
Pushed the pudding aside, the tray straddling
Their thighs while Hilary learned which man to love.

One morning the woman on North Street was dead.
My father made the phone call. He opened a book
And read a chapter and those men had that woman
out of there before Heather was hired by a lawyer
Who wanted her, that first week, to work late.

Gary Fincke
ED 37

IT'S TOO BAD

It's too bad I'm a better friend to you
than you are to me.

I feed you Italian eggplant
with cheese as soft as I am,
and you wash it down with wine
and don't even taste it.

You spew your clever cynicism
and I swallow it like semen,
and I look at you with my eyes
half vicious, half vulnerable,

and you sigh,
and pat my belly,
and turn up the stereo.

Judith Geer
ED 37

EMILY DICKINSON AND I

went walking through the streets of Amherst.
She was in white, of course,
and I wore a pair of faded blue jeans
and a worn calico shirt.
"Emily," I said, "tell me again
about the bee and the butterfly."
She only smiled and shook her head
and pointed high towards the brilliant air.
"See for yourself," she said.

Kathryn Howd Machan
ED 37

YOUR JACKET

One night I slept with your jacket.
It smelled of cigarettes
and you. I lay my head
down on that padded shoulder
and dreamed of nothing at all.

I didn't expect to see you today.
"I forgot my jacket,"
you said, zipping it on.
My hair was still
asleep on your shoulder
as you walked away.

Leslea Newman
ED 37

EARTH : DANCE

Apache earth is female,
lying with her head to the north,
her feet stretched south.

Over her white breasts, the lakes
spell the name of her lover,
he of the far blue west

who she can never, never know
for she is promised to the
turquoise god of the sky

and for his pleasure
she spins and spins.

Helen Ruggieri
ED 37

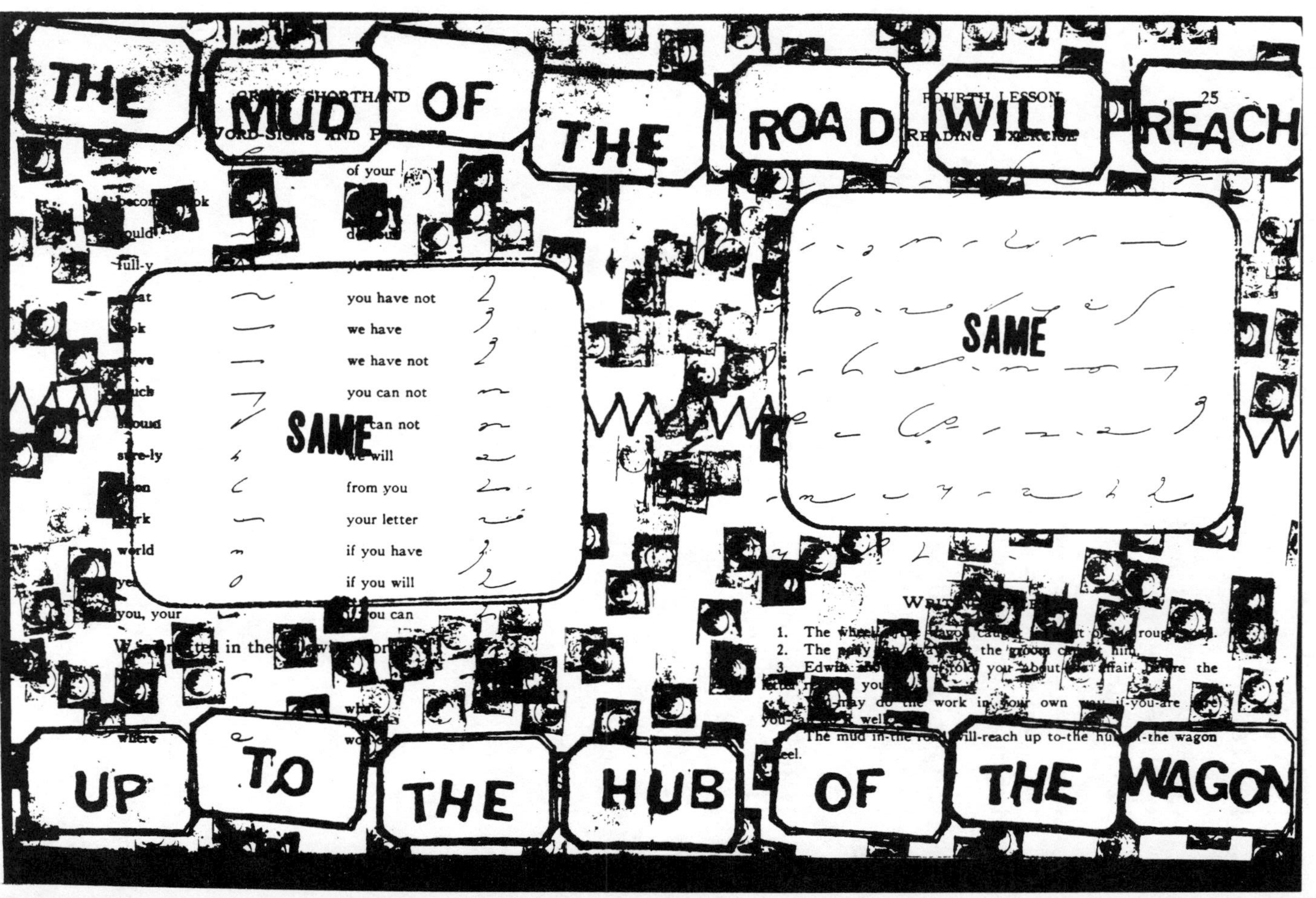
THE MUD OF THE ROAD WILL REACH
SAME
SAME
you have not
we have
we have not
you can not
can not
we will
from you
your letter
if you have
if you will
The mud in-the road will-reach up to-the hub of-the wagon
UP TO THE HUB OF THE WAGON

THE MEETING

They drift in
one by one
Bonnie's on time
I'm not ready
for another meeting
we just met it seems
we never get things
done but nibble, god
always nibbling it seems
we never get things done except
Judi who seldom nibbles has been
quietly getting something
done as usual the agenda is cheddar cheese
and groupthink I think
men would get more done
at such a meeting - what are we
talking about anyway
- covers, letters, printers -
Bonnie is our amanuensis
I am restless
I want to get something done
I want to leave this meeting
and put a coat of latex
on the bathroom wall but
the letter is not written as
Kastle talks to Judi or is it Ryki about
COSMEP, christ, can we
please get something done - no wonder men
earn higher salaries - they do so much
in an hour our letter is a mess, christ,
what am I doing here but noticing that
Bonnie has a silver sheen as
Kastle describes essential puce while
Judi proofs an entire manuscript and
Ryki tells a story with her eyes
which Joy completes as surely as
something's gotten done tonight.

Joan E. Ford